Kissing Frogs

Tall Tales and Insights from the Dating Pond

Kris Anderson

- ❖ Published (2012) by: Dating Pond, LLC
- ❖ 7119 E Shea Blvd Suite 109, Box 451
- ❖ Scottsdale, AZ 85254-6107
- ❖ ISBN : 978-0615678559
- ❖ Printed in the United States of America
- ❖ Copyright ©2012
- ❖ Kristi C. Anderson
- ❖ Scottsdale, Arizona 85260
- ❖ CONTACT: (480) 650- 5594
- ❖ www.thedatingpond.com
- ❖

Dedication

This book is dedicated to all women trudging through the dating pond.
If you are a woman fortunate enough to have landed a prince, cherish him every day!

Table of Contents

Advance Praise

Kris Anderson states it like it is – like it "has been" on her dating journey. No soft-footing the realities that can, and often do, occur in the dating field. Her *Frog Notes* are filled with wisdom, and send the bigger message that we are, at the end of the day, each responsible for how our story ends!

Her oft-times irreverent humor serves to shake up the thinking of those who are courageous enough to dip their feet in the pond and remain ever hopeful that their Prince Frog awaits.

The Dating Pond captures the reader's attention – not knowing what is going to happen next, nor how Kris' amazing sense of humor is going to make them realize they are not alone in some non-so-funny events women experience in the murky waters of the dating pond.

~Anna Weber I Literary Strategist I Arizona

Kris Anderson's descriptions of her plunge into the dating pond are decidedly humorous. The frogs she encounters are eerily reminiscent of many of the personalities and personages women will validate exist in the male world. Women will eagerly pursue Kris' ventures to find Prince Charming; men will read with reluctance, but smile as she adeptly maneuvers descriptions of encounters they find familiar. This read will surely generate many discussions at coffee klatches and in break rooms. I eagerly await another offering by Kris that may include experiences from the male side of the marsh.

~TR Stearns, EdS. | Arizona

I have been happily married to my Prince Charming now for over 40 years. After reading _Kissing Frogs, Tall Tales and Insights from the Dating Pond_, I cherish my Prince even more! My hopes for any woman reading _Kissing Frogs_ : may you laugh, learn, and realize that you are not alone; you **are** that special Princess and when you take time to first love yourself, you will achieve that magical relationship about which you have been dreaming - with a Prince who is not a toad! As Kris would say, "You need to kiss a lot of frogs to meet your Prince…" And I believe you **will** find your Prince Charming, in breaking the spell, by loving yourself first.

~Mamiko Odegard, PhD, Love and Relationship Expert (One Heart One Mind Method™), Author of Daily Affirmations for Love: 365 Days of Love in Thought and Action, Speaker, and Creator of VIP Love Makeover Retreats.

Acknowledgements

A big thanks to all the frogs I have met in the dating pond. Without you, I would not be able to provide these tales and insights. Your behavior, however toad-like at times, really helped me figure out what I truly wanted in a relationship. Thank God for each of you. Really!

A huge thanks to B.E. for challenging me to put my stories down on paper. You pushed me to get this done and I appreciate your words of affirmation and your support.

I sincerely thank the village of people who have gone out of their way to help me launch this book. To Suzette Valle, Karen Gaynor, Donna Newman, Dean Moomey, John Schaws, Mike Privert, Phillip McKeage, Summa Social, Ambient Skies Productions, Connie White, CW Life Photography, Julie Farha, Sandra Miller, Rand Anderson, Doug Anderson, Julie Anderson, Jeannine Boutin, Roger Bernier, Dee Dee De La Mora, Sandi Gershman, Phil Flynn, Bill Crocker, Connie and Lew Archiback, Lisa Mark, Ron Neal, Laura Smith, Andrea Winters, Paula Randolph, Juliana Adams, Deb Duncan, Craig Adam, David Collins, Bob Dickinson, Steve Mora, Kelly Schaub,

Brian Hutchinson, Howard Leisn, Tyler Lien, Elizabeth Hale, EECPA, Smith & Company Bookkeeping Services, Your Premier Team at RE/MAX Excalibur, and Dean Philpott. Each of you is very important to me, and I am so grateful for you enriching my life. Thank you for your encouragement and support with this project.

Elijah and Kai, thank you for keeping me young at heart. May you both grow up to be princes. Z, thank you for winning the stuffed frog that has been my muse every day.

Finally, I would like to thank my mom and dad, Marge and Ray Hackett. You have always supported me and have encouraged me to be the best I can be. You fostered my strength of "activation" and have been the glue of my life. I feel that I won the parent lottery. Mom, extra hugs for your artwork on the front cover. I love you and thank you tremendously.

Foreword

As Founder of the Relationship Coaching Institute, an author, a Marriage and Family Therapist and relationship coach, I have worked with hundreds of men and women searching for the "Love of their Life." Of course women want attention and appreciation; however, in the end - they simply want to love and be loved. Kris Anderson's book showcases with absolute honesty, one woman's journey to find lasting love through her own dating trials and tribulations.

Kris reveals some of the underlying issues that prevent women from recognizing poor relationship choices in the dating scene. In this enlightening and easy-to-read book, Kris' strength is making light of her dating disasters and sharing her learnings from each date through her humorous "frog notes." The author's ability to poke fun and to share her moments of sometimes extreme awkwardness and vulnerability provides a respite for other women who also struggle in the dating pond. She is passionate about addressing just how many women stay in dating relationships that are anything but healthy.

As a relationship coach, I encourage a single woman to learn the art of "Conscious Dating" and transform the way she views not only dating and relationships.. but herself. If a woman knows who she is and what she really wants in her life and relationships, she can find the love of her life. Kris' grasp of "toad-ar" aligns with my concept of conscious dating. Kris' insights will make you much more aware of what she terms "toady" behavior.

After reading _Kissing Frogs – Tall Tales and Insights from the Dating Pond_, it is apparent dating protocol has changed; dating rules have also changed and most of us don't know what the new rules are. In searching for love, Kris shares her dating trials and errors in hopes to help other women learn from her mistakes. Her "frog notes" that can help you more quickly recognize when you are heading right into the face of dating disasters.

My sincere hopes for you in reading this book: May you laugh, learn, realize that you are not alone and that it takes work to manifest the love of your life. As Kris would say, "You need to kiss a lot of frogs to meet your Prince…"

~David Steele, MA, LMFT | the Founder of Relationship Coaching Institute; Author of <u>Conscious Dating: Finding the Love of Your Life in Today's World</u>

Introduction

As of this writing there are 95.9 million unmarried people in the United States and 53% of those are women. Most of these unmarried ladies find themselves in the dating pond, surrounded by frogs, as they search for their Prince Charming. The statistics above don't even include the divorced princesses who are starting over again. The reality of single lady life is that dating is difficult, but the adventures it leads to are funny, terrible, embarrassing, and mind-blowing. And, at the end of the day, a woman must kiss a lot of frogs—and maybe even a few toads—before they find one prince.

As young girls, we couldn't get enough of Cinderella, Sleeping Beauty and Rapunzel. Those damsels in distress were our heroines, saved by the handsome and romantic Prince Charming. We grew up playing with Barbie, Skipper, PJ and Ken. Did Ken ever peel off in his purple corvette with Skipper or PJ? No, Barbie always dated Ken. Period! That sort of planted the seed in our minds that a "certain type" of woman always got the guy. We needed to be "perfect".

With the invention of Photoshop and the billions of dollars spent to attain ageless beauty, we work harder than ever on our physical attractiveness to land our prince. Our distorted ideology—that Prince Charming will save us and love us for our beauty—rules our society. Thus, the dating pond is murkier than ever. To survive, a woman must know the difference between fairytale and reality. We must be cognizant not to project our dream of a prince on a frog that, no matter how well we kiss or love him, is really only a frog (or worse, a toad). So, we date, date, date, date…

I am a divorced woman with no tadpoles (though, I do have two small dogs). Being successful, I thought my "resume" would be enticing enough to attract a prince. I mean, I'm a financially stable, college-educated (with honors and a full-ride scholarship) former tennis professional. With twenty-one years in sales and marketing, I'm a top-producing realtor. I'm a blogger, speaker, and radio host for my show, "The Dating Pond", and I have appeared on HGTV's "House Hunters". My Catholic parents raised me with proper manners, a high drive to achieve, and to treat people well. I own my own home. I bathe every day. I donate to worthy causes. I have served in Rotary Club and volunteer for various charity projects. I have a heart, even though I possess lots of sass and sarcastic humor. I kind of thought I was sort of a catch! But, even with all that I had to offer, it took me 412 dates to meet a knight in shining armor.

Yes, I went on 412 dates in the course of five years! Four-hundred-and-twelve dates with frogs of all shapes, sizes and intellect (or lack thereof). My criteria for a date was: Divorced or single males, kids or no kids, some type of education, some type of success in life, some kind of belief in something higher than themselves, and they had to be taller than 5'11" (because I'm 5'10"). I did not get specific on political orientation, religious background, body art or piercings, hygiene or financial wealth. My initial intention for dating was to meet people without having a long checklist of super-high expectations.

For the record, my definition of a "date" is a planned, face-to-face meeting. Also for the record, dating does not mean screwing. I titled the book Kissing Frogs, but I can tell you right now I have not kissed 412 frogs. Some of my dates lasted all of five minutes, and many more ended with only a handshake or hug. Out of 412 dates, only three frogs made the cut to a second date. Actually, one of those three made it over a month, and the other two frogs made the "relationship cut", which I define as six months or more. I know, the odds sound terrible. Those odds may even depress you (they had that effect on me at times), but putting you into a state of despair is not the intention of this book. My true opinion, after all this, is that dating is a numbers game. If I had to go through 412 dates again, the guidelines I offer you (which are outlined in Chapter 9) would have been my "screening" filter prior to meeting face-to-face.

Most of the chapters in this book will give you a glimpse of the dating scene from my point of view. I've even included a chapter from a man's perspective to give you an idea of what a guy might really want from his potential princess. Some chapters reveal my actual dating experiences with frogs. You would think there would be 412 chapters, but many of the dates I went on were not long enough to fill a paragraph, let alone a full chapter. The frogs' names have been changed to protect their identities, and their dismal dating habits. But I sincerely appreciate these frogs, because they ended up giving me a seventh sense I call "toad-ar". "Toad-ar", toad radar, is the ability to sense when a date possesses behavior that ruins any long-term potential. And, to be fair, I'm sure some of those frogs thought I was a tad too "high-octane" for their needs. I am anything but perfect, but pretty close. HA!

I'm sharing the pathetic dates I've experienced and witnessed with you because perhaps you:

- ❖ Need a little laugh;
- ❖ Are experiencing a terrible dating situation right now and need reassurance to jump back into the dating pond;
- ❖ Perhaps you need to burn your fairytale books and come to the conclusion that no prince is perfect;
- ❖ Perhaps you are in a good relationship and this book will remind you how lucky you are;
- ❖ Perhaps you will realize that the frog you are with right now is truly a prince;

- Perhaps you are a parent and you want to smack some sense into your daughter's warped idea of dating; or
- You just like to read.

The *Frog Notes* at the end of each chapter are my own little "Confucianisms" for women in the dating pond. They are my "words for the wise". The *Frog Notes* are not meant to be preachy, rather "catchy" and simple lessons. We spend hours and hours educating ourselves on finance, sales and marketing, or social media, but many of us have not spent much time on what to look out for and how to navigate the dating world. My *Frog Notes* guided me, and I hope they will guide you or perhaps push you in a different direction if your date is truly a toad.

For those of you still knee-deep in the dating pond, please allow me to suggest that you read my book and immediately:

- Get out of your house and start meeting frogs.
- Let go of the fairytale ideology that may be messing up your head.
- Love who you are and what you have to offer.
- Get your dating guidelines down on paper.
- If you develop "toad-ar", use it.
- Quit projecting princely attributes onto a frog that has no hope of living up to your princely expectations.
- If you are on a bad date, be brief and be kind, but get out quickly.

❖ If you are currently with a frog or toad, get out now.

And, most importantly, remember there are plenty of frogs in the pond. Never give up. One of those frogs is truly your Prince Charming.

PS: If you have dating stories you would like to share, send me an email at kris@thedatingpond.com or visit my website, www.thedatingpond.com. I would love to interview you on "The Dating Pond" show, or share your story in my blog or future books. Your stories and insights need to be shared with other people. Let's talk. You need to be heard!

So, Now What?

The walls seemed to have closed in on me. Three months after my divorce was finalized and my house was still sparsely decorated due to the division of property from our settlement. The appearance of my home reflected how I felt—somewhat empty. So much was gone and I had yet to figure out how to replace what was missing. It was a rough learning curve. Divorce usually is.

My first misstep was that I opted to be my own attorney for what was supposed to be an "amicable" divorce. Mind you, I didn't have a law degree and soon realized why attorneys charged so much (negotiating a divorce feels a little like Chinese water torture). I had survived a year of counseling with a great psychologist, trying to stay positive while going through this special hell. I had lived through my spouse's attempt to hire an attorney in his quest for "spousal maintenance", and groveling back to the judge twice for my final decree because I was missing one piece of paper needed to finalize my divorce.

I really didn't like being my own lawyer, and was happy I majored in Communications in college and skipped law school. I love my career in real estate. I love to challenge my mind, problem solve, and earn money. My workaholic behavior was one of the reasons my ex had problems with me. He would complain that I would hide in my work to avoid social situations. Quite frankly, if I hid in my work, it was to avoid dealing with the problems in my marriage. And, yes, it was easy for me to lose myself in my job. So, if I didn't want to be single forever, I was going to have to make time away from my career to enter the dating pond...and that was going to be a challenge.

The questions that kept me frozen were:

- How do I go about dating again when I have been in a monogamous relationship for over seven years?
- How do I act?
- What do I say?
- Where do I go to find a date?
- What do I wear on a date?

It was enough to make me not want to date. Being curious by nature, I thought I would research all I could on modern-day dating. I scoured the internet, purchased a cornucopia of self-help books, and read endless magazine articles. I attended lectures on the subject of being single (like we needed to be lectured on that) and listened to my single friends' advice. And here is what I learned:

ADVICE: The definition of dating: "A form of courtship consisting of social activities done by two persons with the aim of each assessing the other's suitability as a partner in an intimate relationship, up to and including marriage."

MY THOUGHT: OMG...STREESSSSSSSSSSS. The whole idea of being intimate with someone new? No thank you very much.

ADVICE: From my male friends: "Break out the stilettos and a tight, little black dress. Get ready for some really good and really bad sex."

MY THOUGHT: God, now I have to practice walking in four-inch heels and fidget with a frock that I will never be able to sit down in. And SEX? I cannot even fathom sex with somebody new right now. Perhaps I needed to go to pole dancing classes to get into the groove. Ugh.

ADVICE: From my girlfriends: "Kris, divorce has really helped you lean out. Have you thought about Botox?"

MY THOUGHT: Super! Now I appear as emaciated with wrinkles and the only cure is a toxin that causes shiny forehead. And I happen to like being able to lift my left eyebrow to appear inquisitive.

ADVICE: From self-help books: "Put a vision board together with a picture of your ideal mate. Subconsciously, you will manifest your prince."

MY THOUGHT: Bradley Cooper, Hugh Jackman and Richard Branson will be the perfect cut-outs for my board. I wonder who I will meet that will combine all three babes into one man-god?

ADVICE: Magazine articles: "If you are a woman trying to find a man in dating land, you must be a size one, weigh less than 100 pounds soaking wet; have long, blonde hair (below the shoulders with NO bangs), reverse your age to 30 (better yet, reverse your age to 21), have flawless skin, act clueless and be a D-cup (better yet, a double-D and still be a size-one)."

MY THOUGHT: I am a size six or eight—depending how many chips I eat with my bowl of salsa—and I have short, spikey, highlighted, dishwater-blonde hair. My skin has hundreds of freckles and, at 40+ years of age, my ass is definitely grooving toward the dirt. Clueless? Hell, I am the master at the life-board game named CLUE. I think people could hire me as a private investigator. I possess small boobs and a "sporty" physique. And when I have an opinion, pray that you can handle the heat!

ADVICE: The lectures: "The more attracted you are to the opposite sex, RUN in the opposite direction."

MY THOUGHT: And if I am not attracted at all, run to my car!

I can totally understand why there are over 500 businesses worldwide that offer dating coach services. But, being cheap, I decided to coach myself as I waded through the dating pond. My dating strategy was simple:

- ❖ Get out of my house.
- ❖ Shut the office door and turn off my cell phone so work emails and texts would not distract "meeting" possibilities.

- ❖ Say hello and smile at members of the opposite sex.

- ❖ Dress for success (not for sex), which meant for me: clothes that fit my body, show enough skin but not too much cleavage, modest accessories (not a body dripping in bling); and makeup to accent my smile and eyes (versus resembling Elvira).

- ❖ Limit my love of cursing (understanding that not everyone appreciates the "f-word" like I do).

- ❖ Curb my sarcasm.

- ❖ Watch my intensity meter (I am super passionate about so many subjects and I was raised in a household that fostered debate as a hobby; I've found that not everyone is a fan of debate, or a woman that gets "fired up").

Ok, I was fresh and open to dating. I had studied all I could on the rules for meeting men and I had given myself my own guidelines for navigating the dating pond. I also realized that I did not want my first night out to be alone. I figured I would need a girlfriend to help me on my first night out of my little, single prison.

Missy was my first call.

FROG NOTES: *No matter how much crap you have endured, it is best to open your heart to the dating pond. How bad can a frog be?*

Happy Hour

My friend, Missy, loved happy hour—and she thought happy hour would snap me into the brave new world of meeting single men. It also provided us a venue where we could get a glass of wine and dinner under $6.00 while we chatted about life, love, politics and work. On this particular get-together, Missy wanted to teach me the art of scanning the surroundings for someone hot.

This was my awakening to the singles scene post-divorce. Missy had set me straight on scanning techniques—smile, do not stare at a subject too long and, if I was in trouble, I should cough like I was choking to death.

Missy conceded that, unlike the bar scene, happy hours seemed rather reasonable, usually giving a two-hour window to meet people, and still get home at a reasonable hour. In most cases, it was still light out during happy hour (at least during spring and summer), so we could get a clear view of who we were talking to and, without the loom of last call, we were sure to be sober enough to keep things on the up-and-up.

Missy chose a restaurant close to our homes that offered incredible shrimp and their cabernet by the glass was outstanding for the price. We were enjoying ourselves, and the wine, when Julio Iglesias' double walked in the door. This Julio managed to captivate every woman's attention with his entrance, giving more than a few a case of whiplash.

Julio strode up to the bar and strategically sat next to Missy. He was stunning in a tailored black Armani suit, crisp white shirt and an eye-catching lavender tie. Most men do not look good with shoulder-length hair, but this man did. His mane was probably the best I had ever seen—thick and black with a natural wave that beautifully framed his perfect features. And he just kept getting better. His fingernails were manicured; I noticed this when he adjusted his platinum Rolex. If it wasn't already his profession, he could've been a contender for "America's Next Top Male Model."

He glanced at me with his chestnut-colored eyes and parted his lips into a super-white, expertly veneered smile. He adjusted his seat to maneuver a full-body view of Missy and me. Julio was a pro who had game.

"So, I could not miss these two beautiful women. Wow, look at both of you," he gushed.

Missy was blushing. She was *thrilled* with the flirt. Mind you, Missy was dressed for the dating game—wearing the perfect, skin-tight, little black dress and four-inch heels (she must've read the same books and magazines I had). Next to Missy, I resembled Mary Ann from "Gilligan's Island," wearing jeans and a standard black shirt. My saving grace was the black boots I was wearing; with their three-inch heels, I stood tall at 6'1", and was ready to crush small bugs. I was the perfect wing-woman.

Feeling a bit buzzed after my big four-ounce pour, I decided to ask Julio a probing question: "So, do you come here often?"

Ok, that had to be the worst question I could ever ask. I regretted it the moment I heard myself say it. Missy concurred, shooting me a look of embarrassment.

"I like their food," he answered politely. Then, after a slight pause he said, "I am Roberto. What brings you two here this evening?"

Missy's tongue had suddenly gone missing. She was physically unable to speak, so I had to be the voice for the both of us.

"We enjoy their food, too. And the wine... and the prices are great." I paused my rambling and then introduced Missy and myself to Roberto.

Roberto summoned the waitress over to our table. We noticed quickly that the waitress knew him by name and said, "The usual?" Roberto nodded with approval.

We continued our small talk as Roberto downed his double tequila. We learned that he grew up in Mexico City, was a sports agent who owns five homes and 18 show horses, and he just negotiated a great deal on a new black Ferrari. Oh, and Steven Spielberg and Kate Capshaw just visited him!

Missy almost slid off her barstool. She suddenly resembled a young schoolgirl, immersed in his storytelling and bowled over by his riches. Not only that, she was laughing like a hyena at everything witty Roberto said. She was getting on my nerves.

His second double-tequila arrived promptly and went down quicker than the first. I noticed that Roberto's hand was now on Missy's knee. Missy was still enamored, and Roberto's stories were getting better by the minute. Poor guy—Roberto's pilot had been recently hospitalized, so he had not been to Del Mar for over a month. To add insult to injury, he found his wife of 12 wonderful years in bed with his best friend. And he recently lost his beloved Labrador named "Bear." In spite of the Spielbergs' visit, Roberto was feeling very lonely.

I'm sure you're thinking what I was thinking: Something's definitely wrong with this picture! I slowly sipped my 'cab' as I continued to observe and make notations.

The third double-tequila was taken by Roberto as a single shot. By now his hands were all over Missy. He was literally giving her a leg massage with his left hand and a neck massage with his right. Her body language was not signaling she was turned off, but I could see she was trying to figure this guy out. He started whispering sweet-nothings to her. I saw her face turn beet-red and she politely pulled away from Roberto. What happened to Missy's scanning signals? I was definitely expecting a cough by now!

The fourth double-tequila was slid in front of Roberto. His words were slurring, which is what happens when one has *eight* ounces of tequila in *one* hour. Roberto was feeling no pain.

"Sooooo, Mmmmissy...Mmmmissy..." He was actually humming her name. "Missy, you are shoooow...I mean, soooo beautiful. I want... I want to take you home. I want to give you a bubble bath, and make love to you all night. What do you say?"

I know. Go ahead and take a moment to savor that cheesy line!

Missy was mortified. Everyone in earshot could hear this "one-cent millionaire" bark out his wish for conquest. Roberto's spell was broken, and Missy snapped back to reality.

"Does that actually work for you, Roberto?" I asked loud enough for everyone to hear.

His tequila-soaked tongue drooled out, "Itsh like... itsh... the odds game. If you ashk enough, eventually somebody bites."

Wow. Roberto went from class to ass in about an hour. At least he was honest, right? Being of a curious mind, I continued: "So, if you're rejected here, where will you go next?" Inquiring minds need to know exactly how someone like this works and, more importantly, how we can avoid the happy hour route he saunters. Roberto kindly slurred out his top five restaurants, and we made mental notes to skip them.

Missy had sent me the eyebrow-raise signal of *"Let's bolt out of here now."* I didn't need to be asked twice.

I got up from my seat and smiled to him, "Good luck, Roberto." Motioning to our tab, I added, "And thanks for taking care of us." After all, if he could negotiate a great deal on a Ferrari, he could handle our happy hour check.

Roberto was still reaching for Missy's hemline in hopes she would give him a second chance. She wriggled out of his clutches and we skipped out of happy hour unscathed.

When I got home that night, I felt safe. My little house and my two puppies helped erase the visions of a lecherous Julio-Roberto manhandling my friend. I felt a bit discouraged that this was my first entry into the dating pond. I resolved in my mind that shit happens and that all I really needed was some sleep. Tomorrow morning would prove better. I would slumber knowing I would have reprieve in the gym. Perhaps some dashing prince would be in my spin class at 5:30AM.

FROG NOTES: Frogs that are looking for "free" flies are CHEAP frogs. And if cocktails impair your ability to recognize a toad, do not hang out at happy hour.

The Gym

Many friends had said, "Get fit and flirt," but I thought of my gym as my solace—my sanctuary. My gym offers 80 group fitness classes per week; a world-class spa for facials, massages, manicures and pedicures; squash and racquetball courts; indoor running track; indoor basketball gym; and an Olympic-sized outdoor pool. The parking lot resembles a world-class, luxury auto showroom. I love my gym. It is truly an oasis to me. However, the gym can be a bit intimidating for me because:

Ninety-five percent of women are beautiful. I mean, they could be movie stars. They have perfect skin, perfect bodies, and perfect clothing.

I am in awe that they somehow never sweat and look like they just walked out of a salon instead of a workout.

Unfortunately, some of the married men and women at the gym cheat, and gossip about it in spin class, yoga, cross fit, or at the quarterly mixers. And obviously if they speak about it freely, it must be okay with their spouse. Note: Most of the time the cheating occurs with the trainer, the yoga instructor, a body builder, or another gym rat who has too much free time on their hands. And all of the philanderers have the same complaint: "My wife/hubby does not pay enough attention to me."

The fewer clothes on the body, the more you should BEWARE. From my humble observance, if they need to take off their shirt to show off their muscles or midriff, they want to be noticed. They love attention; and that can be exhausting!

Spin class is the place where I can work out for one hour with no distractions. There, I am in the ZONE. The room is dark, there are 40 people are around to motivate you, and the beat just rocks your heart. In spin class, my life is totally good.

Todd showed up at that 5:30AM class and was longing for dialogue. Mind you, 5:30AM is NOT my best time to talk. It's hard enough waking up, lacing up shoes and skipping coffee to skid into class. I am absolutely a mute until 7:00AM, and the last thing I do at the gym is "dress to impress".

Picture me in my athletic attire (comprised of yoga pants and a t-shirt) and bed-head. I have never been able to understand the women at the gym, dolled up with color-coordinated outfits, caked-on makeup, perfume and perfectly coifed hair. Do not get me wrong, these simply women exude beauty and barely perspire. I SWEAT when I work out. I put towels all over my bike just to protect my neighbors from projectile drips. I come to the church of spin to work out as a loyal disciple, to pedal hard and fast, not to flirt or chitchat.

Todd meant well, though. He had been to over a dozen classes before we ever spoke. But, I had to admit, I'd never even seen Todd before that day; I am just too focused there to notice anyone. In fact, when class ends, I am the first one to bolt out, "See ya!" I am cordial, but I have other things to do... like get coffee. It even took me three years to finally bond with my "evening spin buddies", to slow my roll enough to get to know those people, who have become good friends. So, I never saw the gym an inlet of my dating pond.

"Hello, Spin Neighbor!" Todd chirped with his big smile.

I think I grunted back.

"I've seen you many times in class and thought I would finally introduce myself. I'm Todd."

"Hi. I'm Kris." The fewer words from me the better; my eyes glanced up to the clock—it read 5:25. Damn, five more minutes to go. Todd was just a bit too chipper for this early hour. One thought after another ran through my mind.

"I like the way you push yourself in here. And I love your high energy. You seem to always have a smile on your face. Do you ever ride outside?" Todd inquisitively asked.

"No," I exhaled.

Todd continued, "Well, I'm going to do a 50-mile ride on Saturday. Would you want to join me and then maybe go out for a good breakfast? We could meet in the parking lot here, say 7AM?"

The clock seemed to have stopped.

Kris focus! Wake up! Did you hear him right? Mentally, I removed the toothpicks that held up my eyelids and begin to give Todd a glance over:

* ❖ Todd's about 5' 7". (YIKES! Three inches shorter than I am.)

* ❖ He's in good shape. (NICE, but being ripped won't exactly compensate for our height difference. I have a theory that if the man is shorter than me, he will suffer from a Napoleon complex.)

* ❖ His cycling jersey was endorsed by local sponsors. (This meant he's an intense cycler. I am a "rhythm" cycler. Not a good match.)

* ❖ He's probably 20 years older than I am. (Which is too much for me, I fast forward in my brain; when I am 60, he'll be 80. Nope. Can't go there.)

* ❖ And there it was: On his left hand, a tan-line *where his wedding ring should be.* (SUPER FLAG. Married men or men in the process of divorce are a HELL NO for Kris!)

Kris' 100th and 101st Rule of Dating: NEVER date anyone from the gym and NEVER, EVER DATE A MARRIED OR SEPARATED MAN.

I immediately set the tone. "Gee, Todd. That seems like a great invite, but I must be honest with you. I am not into riding outside and I do not date married men. I think it would be best if we just ride in class."

"Oh, well, no harm in asking. I just thought you might be open to the idea," the smooth operator dished out just as the clock registered 5:30.

Ronnie, our instructor, started the music for our morning inside hill climb. I was saved by the music. I drowned my concentration in the beat of the cardio workout. As soon as the class was over, I grabbed my towels, said goodbye to Todd, and sprinted to my car.

Three weeks passed and I skipped into the 5:00pm spin class. This was the class where my "spin buddies" ride. This time period works better for my "social" stamina. I can actually speak to people when I am wide awake. I took the bike next to my good friend, Sara. We tend to push each other for a better workout. Sara and I humbly stare at the beautiful women in the front row. We are amazed that these athletic women can look that good for one hour straight. They possess lustrous hair, flawless skin, incredible matching gym wear, and perfect 10 bodies. They even add extra dance moves during the hour.

Sara's smile was extra big that day. "Ok, you look like the cat that ate the canary. Pray tell, Sara?" I asked. My inquiring mind wanted to know.

"I met a really good guy in yoga class a few weeks ago and I've been seeing a lot of him. I have got a lot to tell you," Sara gushed. I congratulated Sara. She was so happy. So we agreed to talk after class. Sara raved on about her new boyfriend in detail. She rambled on and on about his looks. To Sara, oddly enough, he resembled Kevin Costner. She was impressed that he owned a printing company. He had wined and dined her at the best five star restaurants Scottsdale had to offer a foodie. She boasted about his good manners, opening the door for her, paying for all meals and sending her roses once a week. And he was a "stud" in the bedroom. She was thrilled that his children were all out of the house. And he was a dog lover like Sara, and she gushed about his dog, Binkley, and their visits to the dog park.

And then she showed me the bracelet he had recently bought her from Tiffany's. She continued down her checklist. My ears rang bells when Sara stated, "His name is, Todd."

My head snapped back like a snake ready to strike and I asked her if it is the same Todd from morning spin class.

"Yes… Isn't he soooooo handsome?"

Not once had she mentioned to me that he was married. I was in a quandary about what I knew about him. She had to know, but in case she didn't I asked, "Sara, do you know Todd is married?"

Sara gave me the evil eye and retorted, "Yes, but I really like him. I'm having a great time with him. And it just seems that instead of being happy for me, you're a bit jealous."

Oh, boy. Sara had drunk the Kool-Aid at this point. She had been wooed over by the devil in a cycling jersey and I was now the Antichrist. "I am happy for you," I told her. "I want the best for you. Just be careful. Someone always gets hurt in the end, Sara." And that was all I could possibly utter. Advice on love or money never seemed to win me friendships.

The Todd affair went strong over the six months. She was in a state of bliss. She and Todd would see each other at least twice a week (as well as in all spin and yoga classes). Sara had received many pieces of jewelry from him, along with a new barbecue and an allowance she received every week for her "lifestyle".

As the days crept along, the chinks in Mr. Married's armor became apparent to Sara:

"It sucks to spend Thanksgiving and Christmas alone without Todd."

"Can you believe he is still having sex with his wife after he sees me?"

"He can't even text me when he's at home because she may see our texts."

"Do you think he will ever leave his wife for me?"

I decided I would just be a sounding board for Sara. No advice was uttered from my lips ears on her relationship with a married man. Morally, I could not stand what I was hearing, but for the sake of friendship, I remained neutral. Keeping quiet in this area was extremely difficult for me.

Eight months later, Sara and I were laying in the Shrivasana pose in yoga class. Shrivasana is the best part of yoga. After you have contorted your body for 70 minutes, the last five are spent lying on your back, your eyes closed, heart and hands open to the sky. You take in deep breaths and are in ultimate relaxation. You feel outstanding and, in the quiet of the room, you can hear a pin drop.

Suddenly, the door burst open. I could feel the human tornado spinning into the room. Her voice was as big as thunder as she bellowed, "You BITCH!"

The entire yoga class sat up. We were in shock— a curse word had broken our world of Namaste. I looked over. There, standing directly above Sara was Todd's wife. She was close to 60, short gray hair and huge crow's feet on both sides of her hazel eyes. She stood an inch taller than Sara, wearing jeans, a t-shirt and cowboy boots, looking like a ranch hand. I was pretty sure she was wielding a whip. Fortunately for Sara, I was wrong.

She grabbed Sara's petite arm as she exploded, "You are a home-wrecker! You have killed a marriage that has been going strong for 35 years! I want you to stay away from my husband, you whore! If you even get near him, I will kill you! Do you get me?"

Sara's face had turned bright red, and tears streamed down her cheeks. Our yoga instructor stepped into resolve the matter and encouraged the two women to step outside so that he could conclude his class. Todd's wife was having none of it and told our yoga the instructor to "Fuck off!" Then she barged out of the room the same way she barged in.

I watched Sara shuffle toward the door. Her shoulders were hunched over, her head hung low. She might as well have had a scarlet "A" branded on her forehead.

Sara never dated Todd from that day forward.

Tongues at the gym wagged about the yoga brawl for weeks, and Sara had become known as the gym hussy. Out of shame and embarrassment, Sara missed her workouts for an entire month.

We still see Todd to this day. He is still married. He still cheats. The new rumor is that he is having an affair with one of the spin instructors; *As The Gym Turns...*

Maybe it was time for me to go to church, if only to go to confession for Sara. And, maybe to also check out the church bulletin for upcoming "singles" events. What better way to meet people? Perhaps the frogs in this dating pond would have some scruples.

FROG NOTES: If you and your frog belong to the same gym, be prepared to move to another if you find out your frog likes to work his muscles out on another princess.

A Man's Perspective

Ken has been a friend to me for years. We met in college when Ken was a geek. As great a guy as he is, I've just never been physically attracted to Ken. He resembles Gandhi a little. Along with his good heart, he has a great mind, truly respects his mother and he was the one man I knew who was honored for his service to the school.

Today, Ken has emerged from geek to stud, and is a world leader in sales and marketing. Ken's savvy, smart, fit, classy, rich and FUNNY. I reached out to Ken for a male point of view (POV) on dating because, let's face it—every woman needs a man's perspective to comprehend the male species.

"Kris, watch my mouth slowly," Ken said. "Men can be summed up in five words: Men want to get laid. Repeat after me: Men want to get laid."

I had forgotten how this was Ken's college mantra. Like a broken record, Ken had affirmed what my Irish, Catholic father would say to me at dinner as a young girl, "Boys do not care about you, Kristi. Even if they buy you roses or give you jewelry, they just want to get in your knickers. Remember my words: Boys will be boys and they just want to get in your knickers."

As off-putting as it might have sounded, Ken's dating dogma became my gospel. I would hang onto every word Ken would utter as he lectured me about men's thoughts. I was a sponge for his knowledge. I figured if I could gain insight to a man's way of thinking, I might avoid bad dates and disastrous relationships.

Ken generously offered me his Men's Ten Commandments:

1. Men NEVER see your brains from across the room.

2. Men DO NOT care if you are financially stable.

3. Men DO NOT care if your IQ is over 160.

4. Men DO NOT fixate on you during the day. (Seriously, they are busy in business—you are not crossing their minds.)

5. Men DO NOT really hear what you say.

6. And when you get really emotional and talkative, men DO NOT understand WHY you are sniveling.

7. Men DO CARE how you look.

8. Men DO CARE about your boob size.

9. Men WANT to get laid. Drunk, sober, happy, sad, mad, THEY WANT TO GET LAID.

10. Men WANT to get laid again and again and again. And if you will not sleep with them, they will find someone who will.

I always felt a bit downhearted and outright infuriated with Ken's commandments. There had to be more substance in a man. A man cannot be this simple—so basic, so unfeeling. I am the eternal optimist coupled with debate queen. I tried to force logic into Ken's commandments:

> **ME:** "But, Ken, what if the gal has a great body, great mind, and she is financially independent, and—most importantly—she offers him 'KEEPER' characteristics?"
>
> **Ken's retort: "He just wants to screw her..."**

> **ME:** "But, Ken, what if he's in a car accident and on life support? She's there for him every day, nurses him back to good health and proves she's there for him all the way."
>
> **Ken's reply: "After he is back to fine health, he will want a good romp. And if Florence Nightingale has gained 10 pounds, he will play mattress mambo with another nurse."**

> **ME:** "But, Ken, what if they are soul mates? They just get each other and are right for each other..."
>
> **Ken's smug reply: "Do you really believe in soul mates? Some drop dead, gorgeous woman with a killer body seduces him at some party...forget his soul mate; he will have sex with the seductress."**

JESUS! At that point, I was pissed, totally baffled, offended, and ready to smack Ken.

ME: "Ken, you're meaning to tell me that all men think this same way?"

Ken's grin-and-bear-it response: "Kris, all men want to get laid. It's all about getting off."

Ken shared his dating ordeals with me on a routine basis. Ken had tried online dating, hired a matchmaking service, and he even went on blind dates. His mantra was, "It's just sex." And he would flash his smile.

Ken actually BRAGGED to me about how, in one day, he had bedded five different HOT women.

SIDEBAR: *Have you ever noticed that when the male species tells you about a woman, they always describe her as hot, sexy, attractive, and/or built? Ken's stories NEVER involved some homely girl who resembled a beagle puppy, a woman missing a tooth, or a gal with a less than perfect body. Need I continue?*

Ken told me about his romp with five different women in the same day and I had to ask, "Did you do all five at an orgy?"

"Kris, five girls all on the same day, all in different places," he boasted. "And it was all INCREDIBLE sex. "

He continued to tell me his rules:

❖ Always carry condoms.
❖ Have sex with women, but do NOT indulge in giving or receiving passionate kisses.

- No matter what, limit the alcohol intake. (Ken reasoned that alcohol lowered the libido and he needed to be in control in the bedroom.)
- Get to bed by midnight. (Ken needed his beauty rest. He's a triathlete and, even though he was getting laid, he needed his strength to train.)
- Never call her the day after you sleep with her.
- In fact, wait three days before calling her.
- If she calls you after the "lay," you may want to lose her number.
- If you are not interested in her after you have sex with her, or if you need to eat your arm off the next day, give her a fake cell number.
- Do not introduce her to anyone you know.
- Always go back to her place.

Ken droned on and on about his rules, while I resisted the urge to puke. Ken was serious as a heart attack on this subject, like a mini-Buddha spewing his male philosophy to me. I found his views to be absolutely pathetic and completely wrong.

"Ken, I think we need to see the Wizard about giving you a heart." I sputtered, hoping that would snap this Tin Man out of his rather cynical spirit.

"Kris, you wanted me to give you the straight truth, and this is as honest as it gets. Seriously, I am having the time of my life. I have hit my stride. I am a chick magnet getting laid 20 times a week, and I'm at the top of my career—my life is AWESOME! I am free and having fun. I am the 'K' man," Ken bragged, like a gorilla beating his chest.

I didn't recognize my friend anymore. Who was this impostor? Finally, I couldn't take another word and I ripped into him like I never had before.

"You wait, K-Man," I started. "When the right woman comes along and sweeps all those stupid Ken rules away, you'll see. There will be a woman that gets under your skin. No matter what she does or says, you will be smitten. And, one day, when that woman creeps into that tiny, little tin heart of yours, you will actually miss her when she's not around. You will think about her even when you are making your gazillion-dollar deals. She will wake up with bed-head and bad breath, maybe even gain ten pounds, but you won't even notice because she actually makes your world a better place. In fact, you'll realize she's the person you want around every day, and not just for the lay. And when that day comes, remember it was me who said, 'Told you so.'"

I got up and left Ken there, mouth hanging open. Months went by before we spoke again. I ignored Ken's calls, texts and emails. I didn't need any more of that man's perspective. No, thank you!

Then, ten months after the K-Man burial, I received a voicemail on my cell phone.

"Hey, Kris. This is your tin-hearted friend, Ken. You were right, Kris. (super long pause) I met this great gal and, yes, she is beautiful, smart, and funny, and I can actually see myself wanting a family with her. I hope you will talk to me. Please, talk to me. You are one of my only true 'girl' friends and I really want you to meet her. It would mean the world to me."

Eleven months later, I was a guest at Ken and Emily's wedding. It was a beautiful ceremony with a fantastic reception, but the best part was seeing K-Man have that special look in his eyes when he glanced at Emily. I knew it was not about sex. His gaze was one of respect, love, honor and trust. The Tin Man got his heart after all! Ken had found his life partner, friend, lover and confidante.

Today, Emily and Ken have two beautiful girls. I wonder what kind of advice Ken will give his daughters when they start dating? And will he tell them his Men's Ten Commandments? I'd be willing to bet he'll be the kind of dad sitting on the front porch with a shotgun across his lap!

After learning all I could from Ken, I needed to get out in an environment with two people I know have my back at all times. I needed to know that it's possible to be out in the dating pond without having to score. Who better to call than Mom and Dad? Perhaps they could help me gain some perspective on the dating scene.

FROG NOTES: Just because a frog has "ten commandments" he lives by does not mean he is Moses. Keep in mind that Moses wandered the desert by himself for years and spoke to a burning bush.

Hanging With My Parents

Spending quality time with my parents is something I treasure most in my life. I definitely won the lottery with them. My parents are superb communicators. They have a keen sense of humor, are fun at heart, and both are very street-smart. They have a relationship that most couples would envy. They are consummate companions who truly like and love each other. They are kind to one another, and they still chase each other around the coffee table. When I hang out with my parents, I become a man magnet. I think that magnetism comes from me being at complete ease with myself when I am with them, and the fact they are so approachable.

An outdoor table for three awaited us on the lower veranda. Dad had picked his favorite brunch spot in Scottsdale, a lovely restaurant that had fabulous views of the hotel pool, and Camelback Mountain in the background. It was a spring day, sunny but not "hot as hell," as it can be in Arizona. There was a woman was playing the harp, giving an air of tranquility. The buffet was abundant with shellfish, omelets made to order, various salads and soups, hot and cold dishes... and mimosas which were poured frequently at every table. The people there were high on food and drink.

There was a noticeable pounce when Pete jumped over the upper-level stone wall. Picture a graceful panther landing elegantly on his paws, eyes eagerly fixated on our table. He appeared at our table in what seemed to be a split second. Pete was 5'10" and resembled a clean-cut version of GI Joe with his dark hair and big brown eyes. He was as solid as a rock in body composition, and he grinned ear to ear with his pearly whites.

"Hello, beautiful," he said with a smile. "I saw you from upstairs and had to come down to say hello. My name is Pete and you are...?" He was literally ignoring my parents; fixated solely on me. My dad immediately interrupted Pete the Panther and stood up to shake his hand.

"Hello, Pete. I am Dad and this is Mom. And this is our daughter, Kristi Colleen."

Crap! I was two shades of fuchsia, and I was ready to hurl. I was overwhelmed that Pete had the balls to overlook my two parents. And Dad just called out my birth names to a perfect stranger. The confident Pete continued, "Kristi, I want to take you out for dinner tonight. Is that okay, Dad and Mom? I promise to be good to her."

I was at a loss for words. Pete just asked my parents' permission to take me out on a date. Am I 16 again? Mr. Confident grabbed a chair and began to lay on the charm. Dad was bowled over by Pete's war stories as an Army Ranger. Mom had knocked back a couple of mimosas and found Pete very witty. It all seemed surreal but, heck, if Mom and Dad liked him, I guess I could like him, too.

We went to dinner. Pete never stopped talking. He was nice to look at from where I sat but, in my humble opinion, he was full of hot air and spun yarns that were fascinating, but rather hard to believe. He gave me a very passionate goodnight kiss, and then rattled off dictator-like instructions:

"I may not call you for the next few weeks; I am going undercover in Cambodia."

"If I call and hang up, it's not that I don't care, but my mission may be in jeopardy and I must release the call."

"If I whisper, I am protecting the squadron."

All I could do was nod while thinking, *Are you kidding me?* Pete deserved an A+ for imagination. Did this really work on other women?

One week passed after Pete's perfect 10 landing at brunch and his 100% rush on me with no word from him. After my lessons from Ken, I knew to proceed with caution.

Then, one night after loving on the doggies, the phone rang. A small whimpered whisper flapped on the other line. It was Pete and he was waffling, "Kris, are you there? Hey, we are flying over Cambodia right now. I am on a top-secret mission, and thought I would let you know that I am thinking of you. I can't talk long; just wanted to hear your voice. I would love to see you in four weeks, depending on how the mission goes…"

All I could picture was a grown man crouching in his closet with his cell phone in his right hand. Who knew where is his left hand was positioned. I also pictured his wife and four kids downstairs in their media room, laughing at the latest reality TV show.

I asked him what time it was in Cambodia. My question was loaded, because I knew the time difference between Arizona and Cambodia, and I was eager to hear his answer.

Pete replied, "Who cares about the time? (long pause) So, what are you wearing?" Busted! Panther Pete was not going to get any further with anymore BS about his career as an Army Ranger. In reality, the only military action Pete probably had was playing with toy soldiers as a kid, and he was clearly living in fantasyland.

I was pissed. I flashed back to my original gut feeling about him when he was pouring his snake-oil charm on my parents. This guy was clearly a pathological liar. The Scorpio in me raised its little tail to sting the army brat. "Pete, fuck Cambodia and fuck you. You might think I am slow on the uptake, but you have messed with the wrong gal. I would be thrilled to have this phone call traced and tell your wife what you've been up to." Need I say I never heard from Pete again?

I relayed the sad news to my parents that Mr. Hopeful was really Mr. Loser. Mom and Dad were crushed, as they hoped Pete was a contender. They felt a tad sorry for my situation, but St. Paddy's Day had rolled around. What better way to cheer up the kid but to take her out to a good Irish pub?

On March 17, the Irish pub had been open for business since 6:00AM. We showed up at 7:00pm. Most people could not even see straight, and were full of piss and vinegar. Stories flowed. The band played loudly. Guinness poured freely and the laughter bounced off the walls.

Within ten minutes of landing at the bar with my parents, Quinn appeared. Quinn was quintessential Irish, with red hair, freckles, green eyes, pale skin, a tall, soccer build with a tiny Buddha belly. He was also drunk as a skunk, loaded to the gills on Jameson and Guinness.

In his best brogue, he put his arm around my dad and grunted, "I love your daughter and want to marry her."

Oh, my God! He had not even spoken to me yet he was hoping my Dad would pass my hand out in marriage. Mom started laughing uncontrollably. She thought this gesture was hilarious. I was shrinking. Quinn's eyes were bloodshot and resembled pinwheels. Then Dad nailed it when he put a hand on Quinn's shoulder and said, "Quinn, I would offer my daughter's hand in marriage, but she just cannot handle you." And Dad was sooo right. I wanted nothing to do with Quinn. I cannot even imagine touching the pour soul. He seemed nice but, hell no!

Quinn was stumped and stupefied. He had no idea how to respond to my dad; he was too drunk to even muster together a sentence. He looked at Dad, then Mom, then me and said, "Well, all righty then." And, Quinn staggered over to the next fair maiden. His opening line was similar, "I love you and want to marry you." After enough attempts, Quinn probably got some tail. Mom, Dad and I laughed hysterically.

Months later, my parents and I chuckled at these memories. I also noticed that they squeezed each other a bit more when we shared these stories. Dad said it best, "God, I am so glad we are married and we're not out there."

The reality was I was out there, treading water in the dating pond. The whole process was a grind. I figured I would go back to what I knew best—focus on work and see what the workplace offered.

FROG NOTES: Frogs will often find you more attractive when you are surrounded by the King and Queen. Don't underestimate the opinion of your royal family before you take the plunge with a wannabe prince.

Interoffice Dating

If you work 9 to 5, it's only natural to look around the workplace for your mate. When you work forty-plus hours each week, it's a distraction to observe the people around you. Heck, married men are known to shack up with their secretaries or "executive assistants". The men actually call their wives to tell them at 9:00pm they have "an important brief to get done" (I just can imagine his briefs going below his knees for that deal to get done). The U.S.A. actually condones workplace love affairs. Office parties are open invitations to "flirt with disaster" and set a new standard of dating: Dipping your nib in the office ink.

Interoffice flings happen every day, but I never thought about dating a co-worker. In fact, I would rather stick a pin in my eyeball than to fish off the company pier because I always think about the worst-case scenario: What if the relationship does not work? Then, I'd be stuck with someone I cannot stand who breathes, works, and urinates within a close proximity of my space for a minimum of 40 hours a week. Are you kidding me? Hell no!

If things don't work out with someone I've dated, I never want to see his face ever again. Period!

I do not want to be at the company happy hour pretending to have fun when Jack Ass is five feet away from me. I will never allow that to happen. It just makes me feel phony, and life is too short to be deceptive and pretentious around some guy I used to know biblically.

I have seen company connections in action, and I recall Sue's experience quite well. Sue thought it would be fun to date a co-worker. God Bless Sue.

Sue's a consummate realtor. Blonde, petite, smart and full of fun, she had a fixated crush on Jeff, one of the top real estate trainers in our region; he was a tall, triathlete who could sell ice to Eskimos. Jeff and Sue seemed a good match. Neither had been married, neither had children. Sue was determined to meet him at the upcoming the International Convention.

At the International Convention, realtors are surrounded by great food, free drinks, incredible bands and an expectant atmosphere. The normal routine is to attend seminars during the day and follow them up with cocktail hour and dinner. After dinner, realtors paired out to go to various nightspots for nightcaps.

Sue was eager to meet Jeff. She had done her research on him. The good news was that Jeff lived within her region, so they wouldn't have to travel far if it did indeed work out. Jeff was accomplished and he was on the fast track to regional office. Sue was also successful; in the top 50% in sales. She dressed the part, with her skirt one inch above her knees, a tight knit top to accentuate her curves, and the right amount of accessories to highlight her big blue eyes.

She dressed like a TV news reporter—conservative with a hint of sluttiness.

Jeff had no idea he was being stalked from afar. However, since I was a fellow co-worker and Sue's observer; I could see the hurricane brewing. Sue was determined to land her man.

I say this in an honest moment: Many women, much like Sue, are determined to get their man, and they will do anything to land the guy they have their sights on. Women who are fixated on landing their "prize" tend to be the most aggressive women you could ever meet. They go to extremes to get a man's attention: sit on his lap, stroke his hair, buy him dinner, follow him home, become his caretaker... we've all seen it before, and perhaps we may have done it before. It's not always the most attractive thing to witness.

In her pursuit of Jeff, Sue became a "she-devil." She probably had a great upbringing and did great in school, but she remained "boy crazy" throughout her adult life. And she made it plain that Jeff was going to be bedazzled by her.

Sue, when first seeing Jeff at the party, sent a waiter over with a drink. Granted, drinks are free at these mixers but, free or not, sending a drink to a man is big no-no in my book. But Sue wanted to set the stage. Her next move was amazing. She sauntered over to Jeff, flicked her hair over her shoulder, and then approached him to say, "Is this seat taken?" *Jesus! Does that line actually work?* Apparently, it does.

Jeff looked like a puppy. I think drool actually passed from his lips as he looked at her and her tight top. Such a man! Jeff was at ease with the femme fatale sitting next to him. Sue stared at her target as she flirted at the top of her game. She resembled a shark and Jeff looked like a minnow. Me? Hell, I was just observing this amazing display.

I watched the scenario unfold. Sue laughed at everything Jeff said. He assumed he was funny but, in actuality, he was anything but. Sue was out to score. She touched his leg. Nothing like having a great looking woman strokes your leg and laugh at your dumb jokes (especially when she doesn't even find you funny at all). But, you see, Sue's game was simple: Make him feel good.

Sue nudged closer to Jeff, and I could see Jeff was now smitten. He had locked his gaze on her. Other realtors come up to Jeff to talk to him, but his focus was on Sue. They left hand-in-hand; Sue had landed her man.

Jeff and Sue had great sex for about six weeks. Whispers twittered at the Wednesday meetings about how they snuck into hall closets, empty offices, company vehicles, and just about anywhere else they could be alone for a quick grope. Sue and Jeff were the couple that everyone gossiped about. A torrid office romance that the rest of us were living vicariously through via the rumor mill.

But when you first burn hot and bright, you tend to fizzle out quickly.

At the regional spring meeting, their mood had changed dramatically. Jeff looked exhausted. He had lost about 10 pounds, had circles under his eyes, and he acted absolutely antsy. Sue, on the other hand, had become a drill-sergeant. Her aggressive behavior was demeaning and her beauty had disappeared. After watching them for a while, I realized that Jeff and Sue had nothing to talk about. But Sue had plenty to say.

"Jeff, I thought you said you were going to get me a glass of Chardonnay?" Sue snarked, looking at her empty glass. She nagged Jeff about everything, and during one presentation, Jeff asked Sue to handle a commission objection and all Sue could do was flip Jeff off with her thin middle finger. Wow! What had started off as a great potential love story had quickly soured to a cautionary tale. Jeff was miserable. Sue was intolerable. And the two of them together were down right uncomfortable to be around.

Their relationship lasted another week before our broker summoned Jeff into his office to give him his balls back. With the help of the broker and the management team, Jeff was given the guts to dump Sue. Their words were simple, "Jesus, Jeff. She is only top fifty percent not top ten. End it."

The aftermath of the breakup was the clincher. Realtors concentrated on the Jeff-Sue relationship more than selling real estate. Every phone call, email and waking hour centered on "poor Sue" and how fast-tracker Jeff broke her heart. At a few of the weekly meetings, I actually had to console some of the realtors on the breakup.

After five months of gossip and lost sales, realtors finally got back to business. Unfortunately, it's sad that a company love affair created such havoc. It was sadder still that it cost the realtors and the brokerage sales dollars. What a mess.

Now, I knew for sure that I would never date a frog from the same office, but maybe I could find someone in the same field. With my dedication to my career, I thought it would help to have that passion in common. I had learned my lesson about regional relationships and I wondered, *Could I date someone long-distance—perhaps another state or county? With my track record, long-distance might be the safer bet for me.*

FROG NOTES: *Never fish for frogs off the company pier. But if you do, make sure you have another pond to swim to when the waters get rough.*

Long Distance – Date #10

The ultimate debate on long-distance dating will always be: Does absence make the heart grow fonder, or is it simply "out of sight, out of mind"? After all I had witnessed and experienced in my dating pond, long-distance could be the logical way for me to date. I run a very busy schedule between my work, exercise, friends and family, charity and travel. I liked the idea of planning time together and looking forward to seeing someone. So, dating someone in a different city was attractive to me. I figured as long as two people communicated and made the time for each other, it could work.

I had met Dan at a top-producer conference. We were in the same occupational field, but he lived in Canada. Dan had handsome, Nordic looks. A tall blonde with big blue eyes and super white smile, he also had a better tan than George Hamilton—no small feat for a Canadian. Dan oozed charm. He would flash his big smile, speak in his deep, manly voice and people would fall at his feet. He was the consummate delegator and he played a better dumb blonde than Marilyn Monroe. I could just about guarantee his physical presence could wipe out Rome in one day.

Women of all ages would bend over backwards to do whatever he wanted.

Dan did not speak to me until the last hour of the conference. So, for all I knew he was mute or he really knew how to play women. His opening and departing lines, after exchanging business cards with me was, "I really like your hair. Hope we can keep in touch."

And he did follow through on communicating. In the first two months, we never saw each other, but Dan's emails were long and romantic. His prose could woo a woman to her knees. We exchanged questions and answers on every subject imaginable — family, religion, politics, sex, likes, dislikes education, business and dreams. We wrote thousands of words, and his seemed to exhibit sincerity:

"I feel like I can tell you anything."

"I really want to take you to Europe."

"My mom would really like you."

"You seem like the real deal."

The only red flag I had was that he preferred to communicate via email. I loved getting his long emails that he put such time and effort to write, but the unusual one-sided communication had this Communications major a bit puzzled. He was 47, but had never been married. He did not have any children or even a pet. After two months of emailing, we decided to meet in person for a real date. I suggested that he fly to my city and book himself into a hotel. That way, if our date didn't work out, he would be at a cool resort and I could leave the scene quickly.

The first day I saw Dan in the lobby of his hotel, I was infatuated. It was "lust at first sight". Since my divorce, Dan was my tenth first date. The other nine dates only lasted as long as a coffee or a glass of wine.

Our long-distance relationship began that weekend. For the first few months, things seemed super. We had agreed to be monogamous and exchanged regular emails, texting and phone calls in between our every-six-week visits. We were busy, but we were mutually communicating.

By the third month, there were fewer emails. The long paragraphs had dissipated into short, text-like sentences. The romantic missives I used to receive now read: "Too busy to email but will call you later." Phone calls were less frequent, too, and when we finally had one, I was usually cut-off in the middle of one of my stories with his new favorite line, "I have to go, but I miss you and I'm thinking of you." Texts were even less frequent than the phone calls. And, in person, there were fewer in-depth conversations about life, our dreams or hopes.

When Dan stayed at my house, it was like a tornado hit. Piles of work and notepads scattered around my living room and office. His clothes carpeted the bedroom floor. In spite of having a working dishwasher, he left his dirty dishes in the sink. If he stayed a week, he found it ridiculously expensive to rent a car, so, in spite of my own work schedule, I became his cabdriver. I drove Dan to the gym, to the mall, to his friends' homes and sporting events. He would spend hours tanning by my pool. I had to hand it to him; while I was running around like a chicken with its head cut off, Dan was making thousands of dollars simply by making phone calls while sunning himself poolside. This man was the smartest, laziest man I had ever met.

By month eight, I was finally invited to visit his hometown. His home was, well...how do I describe it? It was interesting. One of the bedrooms in his condo was dead bolted, and he said I could never go in there. (*Was he hiding dead bodies?*) His toilet bowl was black from never being bothered with a good cleaning. He was a top producer. Could he not afford a housekeeper, even just once before his girlfriend arrived? His office looked like a scene from "Hoarders"; papers and piles everywhere. I couldn't believe how successful he was being so disorganized; he would spend 40 minutes looking for a set of keys to show a property.

Dan had no food in his refrigerator, so we had to go out to eat. The cocktail waitress at any establishment we visited knew Dan by name. They also knew his favorite drink and dinner plate.

We went to see his beach house, a place he'd mentioned on many occasions. He couldn't wait to take me there. When he described the "beach house", I'd never pictured a doublewide trailer loaded to the gills with boxes (and reeking of the smell of dead raccoon), replete with two outhouses. Not exactly my idea of a romantic getaway.

By month 12, Dan was using my computer a lot more on his stays at my home. He spent less time poolside, and even his tan was disappearing. When I asked what he was up to, he said he was "analyzing property" for his foreign clients.

More women's business cards popped up when I did his wash.

He showed up on visits to my home with his friends in tow.

My birthday present was a trip with him paid for by his frequent-flyer miles. The trip was scheduled 10 months out. I felt like this gift was a way to handcuff me to the future.

I intercepted an email I was not supposed to see when Dan forgot to close out of his email on my home computer. What I saw on my screen was like a punch in the gut. I felt nauseated and covered my mouth in disbelief. There, in front of me were the same long, sappy paragraphs that Dan had sent me when we first started our long-distance affair. But, this time, the emails were addressed to a Las Vegas "pit boss" named Annie. Their email chain had emerged into a very sexually charged affair. Then I remembered his trip to Las Vegas was SIX MONTHS AGO! Ah, yes. Dan negotiated that if I allowed him to play Black Jack in Vegas, I would be rewarded with a day at the spa. More like, on her back, Jack. I had visions of Annie on her back while Casanova pumped her for more chips.

To prepare for the ultimate confrontation, I printed out all the emails between Dan and Annie, and placed them in a red folder. My blood was boiling and my mind was reeling over all the red flags I ignored, all the time I had given him and all the lies I believed. I resisted the urge to kill him. I had to play this so cool. I had to be composed. I had to put on my poker face.

Dan walked into my house after a steam at my gym. I noted a bit of pep in his step. I poured him a coffee and motioned for him to join me on the patio. I had the red folder strategically placed on the table. I waited patiently for him to sit his big, faded-tanned ass down. I took his wrist and in a shy, demure tone I said, "Dan, tell me about Annie."

He went white. His oversized, beefy legs started to shake. His big, baby blues darted up to the left (the sign of a good liar). I could feel his pulse racing.

"I was going to tell you about her. She and I are…um, just friends," he sputtered.

I stood up, and threw the paper trail of email evidence in his face. The papers flew everywhere. Dan was busted!

"Friends? Are you kidding me? Get out of my house, Dan. Right now!" I commanded.

"But, what about my stuff?" the big oaf asked.

I looked at his feet and realized how stupid those size-16, snot-green Crocks looked on this gutless giant. My fists were now clenched and planted on both sides of my hips. "I will be giving your stuff to charity as a donation, you _____!" I'm pretty sure there was a major stream of curse words that trailed after this sentence. But, at least there was no blood drawn. I continued with, "You have 30 seconds to exit my house."

"But, but… what about my stuff?" a wounded Dan muttered.

I opened my front gate to kick the shocked, shriveled man out. "Goodbye, Dan. And never, ever contact me ever again."

The Salvation Army was thrilled with my donation.

Okay, this was what date 10 brought to me. As wounded as I was, I knew I could not shut down and quit dating, even though I felt like crap. I needed to set some boundaries after all of this deceit. I had to wake up and set some parameters for myself to continue swimming in the dating pond. This gut-punch was not going to flatten me.

FROG NOTES: *Rethink long-distance relationships! Beware when your frog is absent from the pond for too long. You may find him resting on someone else's lily pad.*

Dating Guidelines

A great mentor of mine always advised me to set guidelines for my life. After Dan, I realized I also needed some guidelines for my dating life so I would be better able to wade through the endlessly murky dating pond.

Since establishing them, my dating guidelines have saved me from disasters, wasting time on the wrong men, and kept me focused on my dating purpose. Who wants to date forever? Who loves dating for years and years with no connection? I could never understand the "serial dater" who dates simply to date with no desire for a long lasting relationship. I believe serial daters are numb and possess little or no emotion. And, in the end, the serial dater has no guidelines, no boundaries, and no rules. They end up lost and in search of the perfect person who does not exist. They remain on the gerbil wheel of dating. And quite frankly, over the years, they start to look like a gerbil, too.

Now, keep in mind my guidelines are based on personal experience, my upbringing, and my evolvement level. Every girlfriend I know has her own set of dating guidelines. We often compare notes. Each of us is so different in our approach to dating, but my friends will be the first to tell you that my guidelines are the most brutal. They often laugh at me and say that I should become a nun. And all I can say is that these are "suggested guidelines" meant for me and not them.

Here are my personal dating guidelines. They are in no specific order. In actuality, I have hundreds of rules, but these are the biggies:

- ❖ Take a good look at how the man you're dating treats or talks about his mother. If he hates his mother or speaks poorly about her, run! Run fast. If he can't be nice to the woman who carried his ass in her womb for nine months, then he will never be nice to you.

- ❖ If you meet a man at a restaurant or anywhere someone is serving you, watch how he treats the waiter/server/clerk, etc. If he is rude, discourteous, demeaning, or condescending to the staff, watch out! I guarantee that flippant tone and behavior will creep into your relationship if you continue to get serious with this pompous ass.

- ❖ If the man hates his job or has apathy towards his career, bail. Men derive their sense of worth from their jobs. If they hate what they do, they will never be happy. Eventually, their unhappiness will erode your bliss.

- ❖ If a man is a lost soul, get out now. I define a lost soul as the man who floats from one job to the next, he dates one gal to the next, and he is in search of perfection. He seeks the perfect job, he searches for the perfect woman, and he can never settle down. Often, the tell-tale sign of a lost soul is the over-40 man who has never been married. Never date a man over 40-years-old who has never been married! He is either lost, is a narcissist, or he has major commitment issues. I have yet to see a never-married man over the age of 40 who has success with a long-term relationship. He wears running shoes to bed so he is ready to sprint to the next, best shiny object.

❖ Do not sleep with a man for at least 90 days. Steve Harvey, the standup comedian and author of _Act Like A Lady, Think Like a Man,_ was right about waiting 90 days to sleep with a man. It is not a question of chemistry; it's about getting to know one another before sharing the most intimate act. If you give up the most special thing you can share with someone right off the bat, you're not setting yourself up to be anything special. And I have two more thoughts on early sex: If you bed him too early, he will think you are a "ho," and if he goes to bed with you too early, he is a "man-ho." Do you really want to be a notch in his belt? Just his conquest? Make him work for it!

❖ If you get involved with a divorced man with kids, take a good look at his ex-wife. Is she Linda Blair from _The Exorcist_? Does she still control his life? Does she emotionally possess him? Does she call and text him throughout his day and your dates? If he is still talking about her all the time, if he has no boundaries with her whatsoever, if she sabotages your dates from the beginning, run like hell! Simply put, this man is a wuss and cannot stand up to her. He likes being controlled and manipulated, and she ate his balls during the marriage. Do you really want to be with a ball-less man who cannot stand up to a woman? So, it is best to face up to the fact that he will never be present in your relationship because he is too busy with his old one.

❖ If you get involved with a divorced man with kids, wait four to six months before meeting the kids. Court the man first and see if you like him before meeting his kids. Too often, men introduce a woman to the kids too soon. What if you like his kids better than you like him? The kids have been through a divorce and they do not need to see another breakup. If you do meet the kids, never spend the night. This is just being respectful of the kids so they do not get the wrong impression. If you need to have sex, get a hotel room, go parking, or have him over to your house.

❖ Take a good look at how the kids treat their dad. Are they respectful or are they little Neanderthals? If they don't mind their dad and run havoc all over him, they will run roughshod over you. Never overstep your boundaries with his kids. They are not yours. You have no say in their life. You are a friend to their dad, not their maybe-one-day-could-be stepmother. Spend time with him and the kids, but mandate that you still need one-on-one time with him. And that means his cell phone is off; quality time rules and strengthens your relationship.

❖ Be very leery of the man who communicates only by text messaging or email. Texting and emailing are one-way communication tools. One-way communication is deadly if misinterpreted. If he has time to write and email or grunt out a text message, he can dial your number. If you constantly hear him say, "I was too busy to call," lose his number. If he doesn't have two minutes in his 24-hour day to call the woman he states he is "crazy about," then he is just not that interested. The only reasons you can forgive him if he does not call is: Because he is trapped under a large object that prevents him from dialing the phone (and the object has to be a real object and not another woman); he was in an accident; or he's in the Outback where there are no phones anywhere...seriously. This is the biggest rule to pay close attention to. If he does not call, he is either no longer interested or he has taken you for granted.

❖ Worry if he never introduces you to his family or friends. If a man does not introduce you to his friends or family members within 90 days of dating, he is hiding you. He might as well tell you the truth. He doesn't want to show you to anyone he knows because there's something about you he does not want them to see. Conversely, he could also be dating someone else at the same time and she has met all the friends, and you are his hidden doe. Tread lightly if you have not met his friends or family, because you might be just his concubine.

❖ Beware of the man who is cheap or always has you pick up the tab. Comments like, "Can you believe I forgot my wallet again?" or "How much is the water?" should be clues enough to his stinginess. Don't wait for his idea of a five-star vacation (camping out of his VW Bus). Or to find out your birthday present is a trip to Australia purchased with miles so you get to stop eight times before landing in Sydney (*thanks again, Dan*). These are all tell-tale signs of a cheapskate. Do you really want to live like that?

❖ Look at the patterns of success in his life. What did he achieve in grade school? How about high school? What about in college? In his business life, did he win awards or climb the corporate ladder? Did he launch a product? Has he run a company? Does he give to his community? If he has been successful in his past, he will be successful in his present and future situations. Winners know how to get up after losing. So, even if he has lost a fortune, take a good look at his pattern of success. If he was successful once, he will be successful again.

❖ Never date a man who is separated or married. Either scenario is a losing situation. The man who is separated is gutless. Why can't he just get divorced? You are sharing a man who is still married to another woman. Let's get basic here: He is screwing you because he is bored/angry/upset with his wife and you are just a hot, little piece of ass. If by fluke the married man ends up with you and does divorce his wife, you will always be the woman who broke up a happy home. And do not kid yourself—if he can sleep with you while he was married, he will sleep with someone else while he is married to you. Run!

❖ Pay close attention to the man who loves his cell phone and computer way too much. Does he get text messages after 7:00pm? Is he on the computer after 9:00pm? He is either addicted to porn or is surfing multiple dating sites or he has another girl on the side. If you suspect him, ask him to show you his phone or computer. If he hesitates or is not willing to show you what he has been up to, bolt!

My girlfriends think I am a bit harsh, but I think if more women really paid attention to these rules, they would be happier. They would weed through the dating process a bit more unscathed. Some women are so bitter and no longer want to date because they have no boundaries. After all, dating is a process of elimination. You have to keep at it.

With these guidelines freshly etched on my brain, I was ready to re-enter the dating pond. I knew I needed more time to heal from Dan, but I had to keep going forward. The bar scene would be crowed and loud, but I had to give it a try. It was time to go out with Bridget and have some fun.

FROG NOTES: To navigate through the dating pond, you must have guidelines for your dating life. What do you want from your frog? What are you willing to give your frog? What are your deal-breakers? Failure to plan is planning for failure.

Bar Scene

The whole idea of the bar scene makes me cringe. The idea of scanning the room while wearing "beer-goggles" only to wake up with someone "coyote ugly" is not my idea of a good time. But Bridget convinced me that the new trendy bar with its own rooftop pool would be the perfect Saturday evening adventure.

The bar offered "bottle service", which Bridget rationalized as, "The men who'll be there must be financially stable if they can afford a $100 bottle of vodka." She gave me a full directive on how to dress (3-4 inch stilettos, tight miniskirt to show off the gams, a top that will accentuate the curves, but not slutty— stay classy).

For the record, I don't own a miniskirt. If I wear four-inch heels, I may topple over. And, the last time I bought something to accentuate the curves... wait... I can't even remember that!

Bridget and I agreed to meet in the lobby at 10:00pm. We were both on time (how refreshing!) and proceeded up the escalators to the trendiest bar on the planet. As we approached the venue, you could hear the bass at full boom and top-40 tunes being mixed with techno funk. I could not feel more claustrophobic. The bar was over the maximum capacity and the fire department could have easily shut down the place. The focal point of the rooftop bar was its huge, rectangular pool... and the naked woman trapped in a clear ball floating the pool's surface. Kaleidoscope colors flooded the sky. I already had a headache.

From first observations, I noted that the popular hair color was definitely bleached blonde (that went for the guys, too). Most women would not have to worry about drowning, as they had plenty of silicone implanted to keep them afloat. Most men were 25-40 (with a handful of 55+ guys at the bar sporting Gucci wardrobes and wiping the drool from their mouths).

The prevalent menswear was dark blue denim pants, and a crisp, white Oxford shirt that strategically hung over the belt line, or ghastly Affliction wear. The men's hair was either perfectly spiked or in the unfortunate "Justin Bieber".

And the women? How could they even sit in a chair in those outfits without turning the lot of us into amateur gynecologists?

It was going to be one *long* night, but then I do love to observe.

Once again, I was wearing my uniform of jeans, a black shirt and black boots. My jewelry consisted of silver hoop earrings, a silver bracelet, and silver ring for my middle finger (I like the idea of accessorizing it in case I need to flip the birdie). I was definitely more casual than the surroundings. I also definitely felt like a fish out of water.

Sure enough, Bridget had managed to use her female prowess to attract one of the older Gucci men at the bar to send us over a bottle of Grey Goose. Our "St. Pauli Girl" waitress meandered over with our bottle as her cups runneth over. She sounded like she had just inhaled helium as she squeaked, "So, let's get this party started, girls." She then demonstrated her ability to point like Vanna White and showed us what mixers we could use with our vodka. I decided on Red Bull®.

Yeehaw! My heart rate was up to 200. I had no idea that Red Bull mixed with vodka would be the equivalent of drinking 10 espressos. My eyes were darting all over the bar—I was so ADHD it was blowing my usually focused mind. Visions of women in heels; men in tight jeans; loud music was pumping through my head. *I must focus.*

What I noticed was incredible. I spied a thirty-something across the room in his "uniform." But, I could not help scanning below his waist, where low and behold, there was a bronze chain that hung below his fly, and on the end of the bronze chain were two bronze colored balls. *Are you kidding me?*

I must admit, I was curious. Bridget was completely perplexed, too. She tried to grab my arm in hopes that I would not open up my sassy mouth. Sorry, Bridget, but the Red Bull® had me by the horns. I approached the Ball Boy and he mumbled, "What's up?" He was too cool for words. He assumed that I was hot for his tail feathers. He puffed his peacock chest.

"So, I could not resist coming over here," I stated, looking directly into his eyes. He was now so full of hot air he could probably take flight. "And I just have one question for you: Are those balls hanging outside your pants?"

With a serious gaze he emphatically stated, "Yes."

"So what does that mean?" I inquisitively asked.

"Duh, it means I'm hung." And he gestured like a wannabe rapper crossing his arms like I was stupid for not even knowing this brand of advertising. I smiled.

"Ha! That is so interesting, because on my way in, I saw two guys that had the same thing, but their balls were gold and silver. Why are yours bronze?" I smiled, turned my back to Ball Boy, and walked away gracefully.

Bridget had been flirting with the gentleman who had sent us the vodka. She was immersed in fake laughter and frivolous dialogue. And by my guess, she had put on her beer-goggles. She caught my glance from across the room and she understood that I had overstayed my welcome.

When I got back to my home, my two doggies were happy to see me. As I petted them to sleep, I knew it was time to step away from the bar and happy hour scene and get serious about a subject that intrigued me: online dating.

FROG NOTES: *Bars are best for drinking. If you decide to look for Prince Charming there, put your frog goggles on and turn up your intuition.*

Online Dating

Is online dating a friend or foe? Now there are different definitions for online dating from the female perspective. For the romantic woman, online dating is "fishing for the right man". Her ultimate mission is to find Mr. Right and live happily ever after.

For the serial dater, online dating is a tool to "hook up" with some great looking "boy toy" displaying two or more photos with their shirts off. Their goal is simply to have a great looking guy on their arm and a Casanova in the bedroom. *Note: Tattoos are accepted.*

For the married woman, she is in it for the affair. The married woman is bored with being the housewife, supermom or superwoman, and needs to inject passion and thrills (and unadulterated sex) into the picture. Yes, men, wives cheat, too!

For the realist, online dating eliminates the hassle of trying to find Mr. Right at a night club, some dimly lit bar, or fishing off the company pier. The realist knows online dating is another avenue in the process of finding "the one". So, as a realist, I decided that after all my awkward experiences, I would delve into the world of online dating.

"Down to Earth—Seeking the Same" captured my attention. And his photos were not full of red flags. Red flag photos are those where the man is striking a pose in front of his Porsche Boxster, or the photo was taken 17 years ago, or has been Photoshopped beyond reality. Then there are the other winners: The guy greased up in baby oil to show off his muscles, in a Burt Reynolds-style bearskin rug pose (and you have to wonder exactly *who* snapped that photo for him), posing with his kids to show off his "wonder dad" status, or the goofy/cheesy poses where he highlights his favorite hobbies (even if he only did it once, at least there's photographic proof).

"Down to Earth—Seeking the Same" had five photos on his profile, and they appeared to be recent. I could see he had a good smile, big blue eyes, and seemed to take care of himself physically. His prose had no grammatical errors. According to his profile, he was divorced and shared custody of his two kids, was an athlete, owned his own company, liked wine, fine dining, traveling and passionate kisses. What I found most attractive (aside from him being 6'5") was that he was looking to start out as friends with the hope of it building into a monogamous, trustworthy and committed relationship.

I decided to send him a little "wink"—the chicken-shit way of saying hello, but I added, "I enjoyed your profile. Please take a look at mine and, if there is any interest, it would be nice to get to you know you better."

In a matter of minutes, "Down to Earth" sent me an email: "Hi. I read your profile and we have a lot in common. Would you want to meet for coffee sometime? Tuesday or Thursday would work just fine around 2:00pm." So I responded and we set up the date. Note to the wise woman: Always choose a coffee spot that you never frequent and hopefully do not know a soul, just in case you never want to go back.

Down to Earth would be my 81st date post-divorce. By date 81, I felt a bit more confident about navigating the dating pond. I had also set my guidelines. I knew who I was, what I wanted, and what I didn't. And, being a time-miser, I was not going to let anybody waste my time. I was either "in" or I was "out".

The day of the date, I arrived promptly. Being on time is just part of my nature. Down to Earth did not share that prompt quality. So, I figured I needed a jolt of caffeine to enhance my nervous energy. Twenty minutes later, Down to Earth showed up. He offered no email or text to let me know he was running late. (Red Flag 1: Are you serious? This is your first true impression to be on time.) *Ok, Kris, just breathe, not everyone is like you. Give him a break. Focus on the positive.*

While he couldn't tell time, he could use a measuring stick. At least he was true to height. Good. He is wearing ripped, baggy jeans, a blue denim shirt, and his hair seems a bit disheveled. Now I knew what he looked like with bed-head. He was cute, but did not have the physique of an athlete. (Red Flag 2: Athletes typically don't have beer-bellies.)

We got started with small talk and I asked him about his business. "I'm a dog trainer," he answered proudly. (Red Flag 3: The only successful dog trainer I know is Cesar Milan.) Down to Earth then added that he was supplementing his successful career with cleaning pools. (*Jesus, Mary and Joseph!* Now, I know you are thinking I am shallow, but I am successful and I just don't think this dog-training pool-cleaner's going to be my love match.)

He then asked me, "So, do you like sex?" *Are you kidding me?* This was all in the first 10 minutes of conversation. Isn't it a dating rule to get to know someone a little bit before asking a about sex? Weren't men taught not to talk politics, religion, or sex on the first date? *Gulp.* So, I defused the situation and asked him what he does for fun.

His answer surprised me. "I have been really involved in an organization that believes you live forever. We meet every Friday night from six to ten. The people are amazing. Would you want to go with me tomorrow night?"

Okay, true panic set in. *Deep breath.* I pulled the old, "God, I have lost track of time. I have to go. It was nice to meet you, but I don't think the eternal life organization thing is going to do for me. I appreciate your time and wish you the best on Match!"

In spite of my brush off, he insisted on walking me to my car. I quipped, "Look, I'm a boxer, I'll be fine. No worries in walking me to the car." I offered my hand for a handshake, "All the best to you." I think my courteous blow off offered me a graceful exit and that would be that. Oh, how I hate being wrong.

Hours after exiting the scene, I got a text from Down to Earth: "Hey, I like u. What are u wearing? Maybe I can come over and cook u dinner?"

No response from yours truly. I was appalled. It had been five hours and he did not get that I had given him the brush-off. Five minutes later, he sent me another text. This time, the text included a photo of his penis. Really! I cannot make this stuff up. His little man was standing at attention with a caption: *See what you do to me?*

Are you serious? What man text messages a woman a photo of his penis? How could that possibly be attractive to a woman? And especially after a coffee date that lasted less than fifteen minutes? I wondered if Down to Earth would text a picture of his family jewels to his own mother.

I responded this time, and did so in capital letters: *LOSE MY NUMBER NOW!!!!!*

And all I can think is that Down to Earth is really from another planet!

Next!

In all seriousness, I think it is time to get back to my moral compass. The church has a singles bulletin. And I noted that they also have singles get togethers. Maybe that will be the ticket.

FROG NOTES: *Frogs often look like princes online. They have spent hours on their resume and have airbrushed their photos. If warts appear on the first date, best to let go and move forward.*

Singles at Church

Every congregation tries to play "matchmaker" and provide a safe environment for people to find their next love... while trying to increase membership. For many, their place of worship provides comfort and gives them the idea that they may meet someone with compatible morals. The rationale becomes, "If a person goes to worship on a regular basis, he or she must have a strong character."

After I had witnessed the "lost souls" at happy hour, the gym, and penis texting, the church singles scene seemed, in theory, to be logical place to go. Heck, these guys are "do-gooders," they genuflect and go to confession. The idea of meeting someone with a high moral compass was very attractive to me. And, if they put God/Buddha/Jesus/Allah above themselves, that seemed to be another good quality. So attending one singles dance at church was not so off base. And I was ready to go alone to the dance. No more sidekicks.

But, what do I wear to a church singles dance? That was my biggest question. I was troubled. Do you dress like you are going to church? Heck, Pastor Gene would probably be there. Four-inch Jimmy Choo's might come off a bit risqué. Anything low-cut and one would get the wrong impression. And jeans only lead to one thing—comfort. My 16 years of Catholic school crept into my psyche as I prepared to go to the dance. Flashbacks of nuns and priests and saddle shoes filled my head. But, I was willing to dip my toe in this part of the dating pond. Let the fisherman's net be thrown into the sea (okay, I agree, way too biblical, but you get the idea).

The Social (as the Catholics phrase it) took place in the Parish Hall at 8:00pm sharp. I arrived at 8:30 to be fashionably late, and to avoid appearing super eager. Obviously, there was an active "singles committee" that planned and organized the big event. The theme was "Black and White." Tunes blared from the DJ spinning 80s tunes, like Michael Jackson, Duran Duran and Adam Ant. Streamers fell from the ceiling, white linen tablecloths draped the tables of eight, centerpieces consisted of black and white floating candles in large, water-filled bowls, and a disco ball hung over the center of the dance floor. Walking into the Parish Hall felt like I was entering Jonah's belly. The overpoweringly big room was slightly dark, illuminated only by the candles. Candlelight always meant that people look better than they do in the harsh light of reality.

And, gasp – only 20 people were there!

My sleuth eyes scanned the entire population: 15 women and 5 men; not very good odds here.

From a quick observation:

❖ Five of the women are over 50. They look really good and are dressed conservatively (defined as covering their ass and their tits so that they do not get sent to Hell).

❖ Ten women are over the age of 35. Once again, they look good. Not homely at all. From where I stood, they took really good care of themselves. They were ready for a "meet and greet."

Now the five pieces of meat—I mean, five men:

❖ Bachelor #1: Bald, pushing 60, wearing a leisure suit. He resembled an older version of the Professor from "Gilligan's Island". He probably enjoys quoting Shakespeare.

❖ Bachelor #2: Short, round and had a very red nose. Definitely an Irishman; looking as though he had hit the sauce before entering the building.

❖ Bachelor #3: Young man, probably early 30s. He was lean and tall, and he appeared to be absolutely uncomfortable. He looked like he might leap out of his skin if any of the 15 piranhas staring at him actually said hello.

❖ Bachelor #4: A gentleman in a wheelchair who had recently been released from the Burn Unit. I had no clue how old he was and avoided making eye contact because I was afraid he might think I was staring.

❖ Bachelor #5: Forty-something, jeans, loafers. He seemed relaxed. Preppy, and had good posture.

Yikes! Where's the punch bowl? Always one to be prepared, I had my airplane-sized Frog's Leap Cabernet in my purse to dump into my glass just in case the congregation just poured Tang. The pickings were slim, but one must mingle. I decided that Bachelor #5 was probably my safest bet. I'm in sales, so approaching someone and starting a conversation is just the nature of the beast within me. I introduced myself and I learned his name was Noah—very appropriate for Catholic singles.

"So, Noah, have you ever been at the singles event before?" I inquired.

"Sure have, Kris. I've attended four in the last year," Noah puffed as though it was the best thing since slice bread.

"Wow, any love matches?" I eagerly awaited his response.

"No love matches but, you know, lots of action. You Catholic girls..." he giggled. His nostrils flared as his "inner demon" emerged from his boyish body.

Did he just say, "You Catholic girls..."? Noah's insinuation that all Catholic girls put out made my skin crawl. His insult made me think of my days in high school when people pegged you for your exterior. Noah had grouped me into the 'all' category and insulted my female creed. I could not let that go. I wanted to push Noah's ark... or at least his buttons.

"So, Noah," I quipped, "define 'lots of action'."

Noah bragged, "Kris, these women are desperate. This is the best odds-game for a church-going guy. Look at the women to men ratio." And then he pointed to victim #1.

"Now, take Maggie there," he said. "She wears the turtleneck and the skirt below her knees, but she is an absolute freak in the bedroom. God bless her."

I was feeling ill. All I could think was this guy was the poster-child for "First in Church, furthest from God." His moral compass was buried three feet below his mattress. And worse, he broke the gentleman's promise of "Never kiss and tell!"

"And how about Mary Ellen," Noah said, pointing to a very attractive woman who was sitting at one of the rounds by herself. "She's a mother of five. Just get Mary Ellen liquored up and she howls like a coyote. She desperately wants a man to be the future father of her children. She told me her husband just took off one morning." The more Mr. Preppy talked, the more repulsed I got. The pervert!

"And Betty over there," he said with a gesture. I looked over to the punch bowl. Betty was taking a sip from her cup. She was about 5'8', slender, and seemed rather refined and dignified. "I've done her, too." Noah was the male 'ho' of the church.

"Wow, Noah. It's obvious that you are quite the church ladies' man," I stated curtly, then added, "I wish you luck in all your conquests. God bless you." I walked away. Good riddance. I meandered over to the punchbowl next to Betty, poured a bit of the punch into her glass and I emptied my miniature Leap's Frog Cabernet into mine.

I took a swig. "So, I hear your name is Betty," I smiled.

Betty demurely responded, "Yes. How did you know that?"

"Noah, mentioned your name," I added, pointing to Noah. Actually, I wanted to see if I could stir up some whoop-ass so Betty would throw a punch in Noah's face.

Betty's voice got louder, "That man is a freak. He's a user. He just manipulates women for his own satisfaction. Jesus will never forgive him and he will never sit next to our Father in Heaven."

I took another swig of my spiked punch. I looked for an escape route. Alas, I was saved by Junior.

"Hi, I'm Adam." It was Bachelor #3. I said hello back and introduced myself. I was now up close and personal. Adam could not have been older than 28. "You seem like a pretty confident woman. I've been watching you and you've managed to meet two people already at this very small event. Do you think you are saved?" Adam asked eagerly awaiting my reply.

"Adam, all people are saved," I stated emphatically.

Adam then stepped up on top of his soap-box. "Not true, Kris. Take the scriptures. One must find the Grace of God to be saved. Not all are truly saved." Adam then quoted every bible verse known to man to back his point. My eyes rolled back into my head. My head hurt. This was a buzz kill. I interrupted the evangelist.

"Adam, I see somebody I know. Can we continue this conversation at a later time?" I asked. I knew damn well the next time I would speak to Adam would be when I made it to heaven after years of purgatory. I sheepishly moved over towards Mary Ellen, the mother of five.

"Hi, Mary Ellen. Do you remember me?" She looked at me dazed and confused. I continued the charade, as Adam peered at us with his dogmatic eyes.

"I'm Kris Anderson. I sit behind you in church," I smiled. God, that was pretty good. Mary Ellen definitely did not have eyes in the back of her head. It is obvious she had never recognized me at church. She stared at me, shrugged and said, "Hmmm...perhaps."

Whew, I was saved. I made small talk with Mary Ellen and noticed five more people had entered the hall—four more women and one lowly man.

Bachelor #6: Seventy, with a walker and Pat Boone-white shoes. His hair matched his footwear.

I was 30 minutes into the singles church scene and the night was rapidly deteriorating. Then, I saw him coming.

Bachelor #4 wheeled himself over for a chat. He was wrapped in a blanket and was wearing dark gloves. He had suffered burns over 80% of his body. My awkwardness got the best of me. Should I look at his eyes, the ceiling or the floor?

"Hello, my name is Chris," he said confidently. "I thought I would come over and say hello and tell you that you brighten up a room."

"Thank you, Chris," I said, "My name is Kris as well, but with a 'K'." I was amazed at Chris' courage to be at the mixer. He exhibited initiative and his smile was infectious. He had a very calming demeanor and possessed the power of engaging dialogue. I knew I had a friend connection with Chris.

We talked for an hour. Our conversation topics jumped around. We chatted about how awkward this singles dance was, and how dating was awkward in general. I asked about how he got burned and what it was like for him to date now. Then, after we shared some of our favorite crazy rules of the Church, we made observations about the people at the singles dance. Comedic commentary included.

By the end of the night, the outcome was not what I had intended. I went to the singles dance to meet a potential date. By 10:00pm, the dance had grown to about 120 people, but I was no longer interested. While I hadn't found a love match, I had gained a new friend.

Despite gaining a friend at the dance, I really felt discouraged with the church's singles scene. Were good men really this hard to find? Did they always brag about their conquests? Did they even possess manners? I was in a predicament. I wanted to go out and meet people, but I really did not have a good grasp on the male perspective on dating. I needed to know more about the male psyche. Perhaps my friend, Ken, could give me a crash course on dating and lead me down a better dating path.

FROG NOTES: Not all Frogs are Princes, but they aren't all toads either. Be open to sharing the pond with a frog who might just become a great friend

The Grocery Store

Who'd have ever thought the grocery store would be a great pickup joint? Never in my wildest dreams would I have imagined getting "dressed to impress" for anyone at my local AJ's. Heck, yoga pants and my workout wear are my standard attire for strolling down those aisles. But, according to both my female and male friends, the grocery store is better than the bar scene for meeting people. So, of course, now I make sure I bathe and dress myself before I mosey out to the store.

Like the bar scene, the grocery store is a cornucopia of people. Who knew there's a grocery protocol? My friends told me to focus on four key aisles when scanning the market for new friends: cheese, wine, meat and produce. There's also a dress code for grocery story flirting: Wear a skirt or dress, no pants, no jeans, and definitely NO SPORTSWEAR. According to my friends, these are the guidelines to great grocery store hunting:

You must have a good question for each aisle.

- ❖ If you are in the produce section, a good question would be: "Can you tell me if this cantaloupe is ripe?"

❖ If you are in the meat section, a good question (according to my male friends) is: "Would you go New York or Filet Mignon?"

❖ If you are in the wine section, a good question would be: "Have you tried this Pinot?" (Make sure you are holding a Pinot over $50. This question then serves a dual purpose: You'll find out if the man can afford wine and if he even likes wine.)

❖ If you are in the cheese section, a good question would be: "Would you recommend this Brie or this Manchego?"

❖ If you find a catch, make sure to casually bump into him on aisles 3, 7, and 10. Act oblivious and pretend it is just a coincidence, then state coyly: "We have got to stop running into each other like this."

❖ Smile… Smile… and smile…

❖ Put a list together of hard-to-find items in the store so you can ask a potential date to help you look for. Make sure one of the items cannot be found so that you can spend more time with your new grocery date. Examples of good items: Champagne vinegar, whole chipotle peppers, spaghetti squash, gruyere cheese, duck pâté, Louis XIV cognac.

❖ If you are wearing heels, make sure to drop something so you have to bend over to pick the item up.

My perspective on my friends' guidelines:

❖ Jesus! Some of these rules are RIDICULOUS!

- ❖ I know that some of those corny questions will never be uttered from my lips.

- ❖ I am never going to drop something and do a "bend and snap" move from *Legally Blonde*. The whole thought of "bend and snap" is equal to "bend and barf" to me.

- ❖ One must work with their true personality and, by God, I have attitude and sass. But, I do like the idea of having the Louis XIV Cognac on the list

- ❖ Smiling will not be hard at all. I might even be laughing...to myself. Hell, I probably will look like the female version of the Joker as I try to act couth.

So, I walked into my favorite grocery store with clear guidelines. I felt like I was dressed for success. My mantra was: Let the games begin! Keep in mind, when I normally shopped, I had a list in hand, wearing sneakers in sprint mode and my whole goal was to get in and out of the store in less than 15 minutes. Saunter was not the choice vocabulary for this intense Scorpio.

The cheese section and bakery looked like a ghost town. The only "hot" commodity was the 80-year-old man behind the counter. There was absolutely no way I would ask him, "Is this cheese semi-soft or hard?" Strike One.

I slowly wheeled down Aisle One which was another joke—there were four women who were also "dressed to impress". Boredom was overcoming me. I tried to enthusiastically stare at the various bottled waters and pretzel bags. A yawn overtook my face.

Aisle Two had two more females. Their baskets were filled with family meal ingredients. I read the various spices on the shelf. I was amazed at the price of steak rubs. Strike Two.

On Aisle Three, we had a man! But, he was 75 and shopping for toilet paper.

Aisle Four was empty. It was the shampoo and toothpaste aisle. I was tempted to take a swig of Scope. Minty fresh breath was about all the excitement this place held.

At the end of Aisle Four, I wheeled into the meat department. There were five folks in line with their number tickets. I took count: two men and three women. Both men were middle aged and wore the "eternal ring". Married. In fact, the wives were in tow and I heard the one couple argue over, "Pork shoulder or rack of lamb." As their voices escalated in anger towards each other, I wanted to blurt out, just get both! Strike Three.

Now, I was frustrated. I had nothing in my basket. The last 20 minutes of "grocery man scanning" felt like sharp pins being lodged into my pupils. Patience is not my strong suit. I skipped Aisles Five, Six and Seven altogether. This hot place to meet men was turning out to be a scavenger hunt. I decided to give it one last shot: The Produce Department.

Ding, ding, ding...We had a winner! There, amongst the fruit and vegetables, was one single man (other than the grocery manager who was doing Idaho potato inventory). I made my way over to the apple bins where he was standing. He was tall, fit, wearing loose 501 Jeans, flip-flops, and a green Nike T-shirt that said "JUST DO IT". His baseball cap was worn backwards. I could only think that he was either bald or he had bed-head. As I got closer, I noticed he had no ring on his left finger. In fact, his fingernails were clean, and he smelled like Irish Spring.

I was nervous. What are the rules again? Questions; I was supposed to have questions. But I could not think of a good apple question.

And then he opened up his mouth…

"Hi! I was wondering if I could get your help with these apples," he squeaked.

I could not believe my ears. The Apple Man had a high pitched, Mickey Mouse sounding voice that could only make you wonder if he was once a woman. His big body and his tiny mouse voice were diametrically opposed. I was now holding back my nervous laughter. I needed to get out of this dilemma and quickly. And hell, what did I know about apples? I hate fruit.

I looked straight at Apple Man and I kept looking at him. I decided "Mute" was the best approach. Thank God I knew a little sign language. I smiled and I signed "Hi" to him. Whew. He smiled at me, and I managed to pass him slowly on his left—I could see the cash registers and the exit door. I only had 100 feet to go.

Then, I felt a hand tap my shoulder.

It was Apple Man. He also knew sign language, and was a signer on steroids. He started signing rapidly and eagerly awaited my communication. CRAP, a professional signer! He was probably deaf, thus the reason for his high-pitched voice. At this point, I was so embarrassed; I was a true jackass trying to pretend I knew sign language. I deserved this karma. I just wanted the ground to swallow me whole. I could not sign proficiently, so I just looked at him, I smiled, and I waved goodbye.

The Apple Man was crushed, and I was cursing myself for even thinking that the grocery store would be my next "meet my mate" place. *Jesus, have I lost my mind?* This was like a bad dream. Was I on candid camera? Had I just been PUNK'D by my friends? At this point, the text of a penis picture would've actually made me laugh.

By the time I got to my car, my skin crawled at the thought of my bad grocery experience. I

shuddered like an eight-year-old girl who just caught cooties.

I took an oath for future grocery visits that I still recite today:

Thou shall always wear workout wear, sneakers, and your Titleist visor to the grocery store.

Thou shall create a good grocery list so that you are focused and can get out of the store in less than 15 minutes.

Thou shall not shop for Prince Charming at the grocery store.

AMEN.

FROG NOTES: *The only frogs in the grocery store worth taking home are in the frozen food section.*

Blind Dates – Date #107

After hearing me bitch and whine about happy hour, the gym, long-distance, the bar scene and the grocery store, my friends were on a mission to find me a prince. I will not forget my colleague's suggestion, "Hey, Kris, I have this friend of mine who would be perfect for you." Truth be told, I've always been a bit skeptical about venturing into the world of "blind dates". After all, the word "blind" is defined as being unable to see; sightless.

So, if the aesthetic world we live in is based on looks, why would anyone agree to be "sightless" prior to meeting a date? Even online dating sites encourage users to post a photo for a better response. At least that was my inner-brain debate prior to my colleague's suggestion. What the heck? I have respect for my colleague and trust her opinions on most things. And, how bad could this "sightless" dating truly be?

Paul and I had spoken on the phone just once before meeting in person. He had a nice phone voice and, based on his vocabulary, seemed well educated. He was also artistic; his work revolved around graphic design. Paul described himself as 5'10', with longer brown hair, blue eyes, an athletic build, and said he would be wearing jeans and a t-shirt. We agreed to meet for a drink and he chose happy hour at a Mexican restaurant.

As usual, I was punctual. Punctual is defined as "on time"—not one minute early (too eager) and not late (disrespectful). The Mexican restaurant was splitting at the seams. It was standing-room-only, with lots of silicone, Ed Hardy shirts, and margaritas a-plenty. My eyes scanned the room for an athletic, 5'10", creative-type in jeans and a t-shirt (which should stand out in a Scottsdale bar). After trolling through the standing happy hour crowd, I sauntered over to the tables. Paul had wedged himself between a cocktail table and a pole in the corner of the room. My first impression was that the man had to weigh 120 pounds (his leg was the width of my upper arm). Not quite an "athletic" build by dating website standards.

I don't know about you, but no woman I know wants to outweigh her date. As a former professional athlete, I tend to take that whole "athletic build" thing to heart. I weigh in at 138 and have kept in shape from years of tennis. Paul was a feather-weight at best. For a brief moment, I recalled a story that one of my "nymphomaniac" girlfriends overshared— where she had taken a skinny man to bed and literally broke one of his ribs with her strong inner thighs while in the missionary position. I proceeded with caution.

I walked over, offered a firm handshake, a bright smile and a, "Hello, I'm Kris," as my salutation. He returned my grip with a limp hand, no smile and greeted me with a flat, "This was the best place I could find in this zoo."

Paul seemed perturbed about how loud and crowded the bar was as he tapped his foot while rapidly scanning the room for a vacant seat. I was a little confused. After all, he chose the venue and he knew it was happy hour. Was he expecting it to be library quiet?

A vibrant cocktail hostess greeted us eagerly and asked for our order. Being decisive I said, "I'll have your house margarita."

Paul immediately shot me a look and quipped, "You drink?"

A long and uncomfortable pause followed. "I guess I will have an ice tea," he said and then asked, "Are the chips free?"

Our lovely hostess told Paul that the only way you can get free chips is if you belly up to the bar.

Paul then asked me, "You want to go up and get the chips?" *Are you kidding me?*

I looked kindly in the eyes of the hostess and said, "Please bring us our drinks and the chips. We're happy to pay for them."

Jesus, Mary and Joseph! My blind date had invited me to happy hour, questioned my drinking and was happy to have free chips as long as I was the one to go get them. Briefly, I imagined him as a male "wishbone" asking to be snapped. My wish was easy: *Get me out of here now!*

After our happy hour drinks and not-free chips arrived, we meandered through a somewhat awkward conversation. The only way to keep that uncomfortable conversation going was for me to keep asking him questions. He told me he was a liberal, and that Republicans are stupid and bourgeois. His big claim of being an athlete proved to be incorrect, as he'd been sidelined from working out for the past nine months due to a bad back. He had no health insurance (no wonder his back was still bad!) and he bragged about sneaking into Hispanic "free health clinics" (and, by the way, he is not Hispanic). He's an atheist and, at the age of 40, he'd never had a relationship that lasted longer than 11 months. As he spoke, red flags began flying everywhere!

Paul never once asked one question about me (the psycho-analytics tallied narcissist). Not one question. Politics on the first date is never a good topic and, unfortunately for him, I am a conservative and a fan of capitalism. He had indirectly called me "stupid" right off the bat.

As for him being athletic? Via his verbal resume on our pre-date phone call, he had said he worked out three times a week. Correction—he used to work out three times a week, which to me means he is a "wannabe athlete." In nine months he had not done one lick of exercise since his back injury prevented him from doing much more than walking, and even that was a task. I wanted to offer the "thin man" a pair of crutches. Adding insult to injury, Paul was one who wants to "stick it to the man" by refusing to pay for healthcare.

It occurred to me that he had not smiled once during our date. My overactive mind assumed, if he does not carry health insurance, he must not carry dental insurance so, bad teeth?

As a Catholic, I believe in a power higher than myself. I don't expect my dates to have the same religion as me, but a little spirituality is nice. With Paul being an atheist, we could not be more diametrically opposed.

Finally, and most importantly, remembering that the man had not been able to sustain anything longer than an 11-month relationship in his entire 40 years of life, I began to question, *does he hate women? Perhaps he is a closet homosexual, which is fine, but come out my friend! More red flags waved and I heard in my head, Run, Forrest. Run!*

I gulped my drink as fast as I could. He summoned our glorious hostess for the check. I personally think she (as another single woman) could sense my vibes across the room because our check arrived lickety-split. Paul reached for the bill and pulled out his mini-reading glasses and said, "Kris, you had the margarita and chips and I had the ice tea."

By this point, I was so irritated I flatly stated, "Paul, I am happy to pay. Don't worry, I've got it." I threw down a $20 bill (since I am bourgeois and earn money for a living). Prior to bolting for the door, I said, "Paul, do you know who I truly admire in this day and age?" He looked at me blankly. I smiled and shouted, "Sarah Palin!"

Somehow, Paul caught up to me at the door. He asked me what kind of car I drove and if I needed him to walk me to my car. I tried not to laugh or offer to walk him to his car since I have twice the muscle strength of this wisp of a man.

Because I was raised to be considerate, at least with my outer voice, I smiled and said, "No worries, Paul. I can handle it from here. Good night. I wish you luck." I refused another limp handshake and walked to my car. As I put my key in the ignition, my curiosity got the best of me. In my rearview mirror, I watched as Paul crawled into his hornet-green Scion, "creatively" wrapped with his graphic design company name and logo.

After this experience, I would almost prefer a deaf date than another blind one.

P.S. The next day I called my colleague who had sold me on this guy being "perfect for me." My only question was, "Do you hate me?"

FROG NOTES: *It helps to be truly blind if you are considering a blind date, but being deaf would not hurt as well. Tread cautiously when a good friend suggests a "perfect" match in the pond.*

Speed Dating

I figured blind dates were not going to prove successful for me, so how bad could speed dating be?

Speed Dating is an organized matchmaking event where you rotate every three minutes to another "mini-date." The short time limit prevents you being monopolized by one person and you meet more people in 60 minutes than you would in an entire year. The organizer rings a bell to cue the participants to move to their next mate. At the end of the big event, you sit down with the organizer to show the list of mates you would like to get to know better. You receive the contact information and start your "courtship."

The idea of speed dating was alluring to a woman like me who is a "time-miser." I loved the idea of breezing from table to table to meet people while not having to be "stuck" for too long. And the thought of being able to "trust your gut" in three minute increments seemed very logical to me; three minutes seemed long enough for me to judge if I had a "love connection" or "mate elimination". Nobody had to know my last name and I did not have to share my contact number OR give out a bogus telephone number—speed dating seemed worthy of a Kris effort.

The organizer of the big event was smart. She hosted it on a Saturday morning at 11am at a favorite, centrally located hotel. In order to get your number, you had to register online and pay a nominal fee of $39.95. When I arrived, 45 people were in attendance, 20 men and 25 women. The goal was to have an even number of men to women. So, the last five to sign up were on a "waiting list" to play. The organizer hoped that five male stragglers from the hotel or from the advertising would show up "last minute." As luck would have it, three more stragglers showed up but, that meant two women would have to attend the next "speed dating" show.

Being new to the game, I concentrated more on the logistical arrangement of the room versus the players. The room had 23 tables for 2. Each table had a sign with a number on it, a pitcher of water and two glasses. No snacks, no flower arrangements, no disco balls, no frills. I assumed the water was either there to quench your thirst or throw at your potential date.

Like cattle being herded for slaughter, the players were given their instructions on the game. Absolutely no last names were to be given; absolutely no exchanges of business cards or contact information. You'd only have three minutes to get to know one another, so be cognizant of time.

"Pay attention to the sound of the bell to make a table change," said the organizer. One ding meant move to the next table and two dings of the bell meant "chat away".

"You have made a commitment to be here today and we hope you will honor the full session. It is rude to leave early," the organizer warned. "If you leave for any reason, you are out and will not be able to get contact information nor will your contact information be shared with anyone."

I decided to dress business casual for speed dating. Black slacks, sapphire blue blouse, and silver jewelry to accessorize my classic look. I did not want to appear too eager nor did I want to show too much skin. My favorite fragrance, Aliens, was my scent for the day. My overall feeling was to be open to meeting new people. Still, I memorized where the "exit doors" were in the room, just in case.

I was handed my number: 8.   According to my Indian friends, the number eight brought good luck. So, I felt good about my number. I was told when the bell rung, I would go to table 8. When I heard the bell ring again, I would move to table 9. Prior to the bell clang, I was beginning to get nervous. There I was, a grown woman reducing myself to a game of musical chairs to spend three minutes with 23 different men. That meant 69 minutes of banter; no bathroom breaks, and only water to soothe the nerves. Super!

DING!

I darted to table 8.

DING! DING!

Sitting across from me was a man twice my age. He was carrying 40 extra pounds (all around his stomach). He was eager and he obviously had played this game before. "So, my name is Charlie. I lost my wife a year ago and I am looking for the love of my life. I love wine, I am a foodie, and I enjoy riding horses..."

"Hello, Charlie. I am #8. I enjoy boxing, I love vegetables, and how long were you married?" I asked him anything to keep him talking so that bell would ring again. In five seconds flat, I just wanted that bell to ring. Charlie then rattled on about his wife, their great marriage, his kids...

DING!

Table 9. The next man looked like a serial killer. He was wearing a trench coat and it was 75 degrees outside (I thought he might be carrying a concealed weapon underneath that coat). He possessed dark, brooding eyes, a very fair complexion, slicked black hair and a scar below his chin (I wondered if it was a knife wound). He did not smile, and he was super shy. He just stared at me. Great, now I felt obligated to talk, but I didn't. Serial Killer and I just stared at one another. I chalked it up to grade school when my friend and I would see which one of us would blink first. I would make this into a game.

We sat three minutes without speaking. Neither of us flinched.

DING! DING!

Whew, a huge sigh of relief. I thought 8 would bring me luck, but 8 was a curse.

DING!

Table 10. The next guy definitely worked in the pocket-protector division for Aerospace Engineering. He had a comb-over, wore thick glasses, had a nasally voice and he probably stood at 5'2". Dear Jesus, I have 60 more minutes of this?

The geek-squad hero spoke rapidly, "So, my name is Ed. I studied at Occidental. I got my degree in Electrical Engineering, graduated cum laude. Honeywell has been very good to me. I have been there for over 20 years… "

Did I just yawn? I was bored out of my mind. Ed recited his life resume to me. His lips kept moving, but I had zoned out. Why had the organizer choose three minutes for each round? If it were my game, I would make each round five seconds long. In fact, I knew what was missing from each table: there should be a gong instead of the pitcher of water. If you were bored or if someone was a dud, you could gong them. I smiled at the thought of gonging Ed.

Now in all fairness, I was sure Ed thought I was a wall flower. I had not said one thing at all. And I know myself too well. If I do not like you, you will know it. I am anything but subtle.

Ed was still speaking when the glorious DING! DING! rattled my ears. I had become the speed-dating walking zombie. I knew I resembled a deer in headlights. My body was numb and my ears were bleeding from Ed's curriculum vitae.

I quickly scanned the room. There was no hope in sight. Not even one male specimen got the Kris "second look." Not even one hopeful contender for these rounds of boxing. I felt like a welter-weight fighter in a heavy weight fight and it was the tenth round. Gulp. Where are these people from? What have I signed up for? I was now convinced that the organizer had pulled people off the street with a sign that said: "Lonely? Jump in my minivan! Speed dating to the rescue."

Table 11 awaited me. But, exit door #1 was now illuminated. Behind exit door #1 was freedom, lunch, and perhaps a shot of tequila.

DING!

I moved towards table 11 and got a glimpse of speeder #4 approaching the table. His shoulders were slumped over from his earlier sparring rounds. He was wearing Wallaby shoes from the 1970s and sported a mullet hairstyle. He could've been the nicest man in the world, but I could not do this for another moment. Perhaps my Aliens fragrance manifested male aliens. One hour was sacred to me. I could be at spin class, I could be meditating, I could be talking to my best friend in the world on the telephone for one hour, but I could not stay in this adult game of Pit for one second more! I totally acknowledged that I was the rudest person in that DING! DING! room. I had let down my fellow daters. But I was thrilled to be free of speed dating.

All this contrived dating crap was getting me nowhere. I needed a break from this organized madness. In all honesty, at that point I figured it would be best if I just read about men.

Frog Notes: Have you ever heard of a princess meeting her prince charming from "speed dating"? Me either.

Divorced Man with Kid(s)
First Date- Date #201

Sixty percent of all eligible men over the age of 40 are divorced with kids. According to many magazine articles, a woman dating a divorced man with kids is advised to, "Proceed with caution!" There are two strong forces that a woman must understand when entering into a relationship with this prototype: his ex-wife and his kid(s).

On the opposite side of this spin, a divorced man with kids provides two positive thoughts: A divorced man was once married so he honored the idea of marriage; he was willing to commit to somebody. If he has kids, he is not completely selfish. By having offspring, he understands the concept of self-sacrifice. He is not a narcissist and that's a huge sigh of relief for me.

After dating the single male, the never-married, and dating the divorced man with no kids, the divorced man with kids actually seemed okay to me. Heck, he probably suffered quite a bit, and reminded me of one of my favorite quotes: "Damaged people are dangerous, as they know how to survive." I welcomed the change. Divorced Man with Kid(s), here I come.

Marvin was introduced to me through a mutual acquaintance. We met at a sporting event. After our initial introduction, we spoke on the phone prior to meeting for dinner. Marvin was at the top of his law firm. Every 10 days, he would travel to Asia for his litigation case. He had been divorced for one year and he shared equal custody of his teenage boy with his ex-wife. He was a triathlete and talked incessantly about his scuba diving watch that could track sharks 100 feet deep in the water. Marvin was 6'4" with a wiry runner's build. His hair was silver. He was good looking, and had dressed in Dockers, a light blue Oxford shirt, and light tan Docksiders. He and I arrived at our date at 7:30pm on the dot. Marvin had chosen the restaurant and knew the owner. We got the best table in the house.

Marvin was my 201st post divorce dating experience; first observations...

Marvin was extremely nervous and seemed a bit shyer in person than on the phone. He immediately started to arrange his silverware, fuss with his napkin, move the water glass, or check his watch. I could feel the vibration of his spastic knee under the table. He literally was "jolting," a bundle of nervous energy. He placed his cell phone next to his knife.

"Kris, I apologize now, but my son may call or text during dinner, even though this is his weekend with his mom. He's meeting his friends for a movie. So, if he calls or texts, I may have to take it," Marvin explained cautiously.

"I totally understand," I replied, even though I really didn't. Didn't he just tell me that the son was with his ex-wife this weekend? Why would the son need to call or text Marvin if she was the one in charge for the weekend? Kris, just give him a break. Breathe. What a nice night. Smile.

I then felt compelled to ask as many questions as I could about his son. While probing, I learned that his son, Tom, was a sophomore in high school, a straight-A student who played football and was the only child. Marvin's fidgeting loosened up as he talked about Tom, he was getting a little relaxed. Then, Marvin's cell phone rang. He gestured to me to let me know it was his son. One could hear a voice on the other line while Marvin kept listening and saying: "I hear you son... Uh huh... Yes, I got it... Ok, sounds good." The phone call lasted about five minutes.

As he hung up, I probed with my sass factor at about an eight. "Is everything okay? Any blood or vomiting?"

Marvin didn't even crack a smile, "Everything is fine. No blood or vomit. How about a drink?" Marvin took the liberty of ordering us wine. I could sense a little tension. I noted Marvin was back to fidgeting. Now he was placing the salt- and peppershakers in their exact spot—definitely OCD for sure.

The wine arrived and Marvin guzzled the Pinot.

Text one...

I could not read it across the table but, by the look on his face, the text was from Tom. Marvin picked up his phone and immediately texted back.

Text two...

This time, Marvin's face went red. He picked up his phone and shot a very definitive text back. I felt his legs shaking underneath the table. He was definitely agitated.

"Is everything okay, Marvin?" I asked kindly. Heck, I could feel my own heart speeding up. Was that sweat on my palms?

"My son's mom is refusing to pick the boys up tonight. Tom needs a ride back from the movies. And she wants me to pick him up." Marvin explained.

"Hmmm... Isn't it her weekend?" I muttered.

"Yes, but she is refusing to pick them up," he barked.

Once again, I popped into logic mode. "Marvin, can one of the other parents pick the boys up and deliver them to her house?"

Text three...

Now, Marvin was ticked. He grabbed his knife and tapped it against the grain of the wood table. He read the text, gulped down half of his wine, and immediately ripped off another text. He was typing faster than Annie Oakley at a shoot-out.

Text four... Text five... Text six...

Then, the phone rang. I felt like I was at a circus. Marvin had now gone from shy, quiet, demure attorney to a snake-eyed Ninja. His voice was elevated. His foot was now tap-dancing under the table. And the knife play was seriously concerning.

"Listen, you stupid bitch! You knew I had a date tonight. It is your weekend. Tom is your son, too. If there is an emergency, I will be there. But, for the last time, I am on a date and you will have to figure it out!" Marvin slammed the phone down on the table.

He resembled a crazed, psychopathic killer. Red flags unfurled. He had called his ex-wife a "stupid bitch" within 20 minutes of our first date. He has shot off six texts and taken two phone calls all at dinner. Jesus, help me here.

I sensed that Marvin felt like opening up. I wasn't sure if it was the wine that had kicked in or if he just needed to vent. He now decided to treat me as his new psychologist.

"Kris, Sandy and I were married for over 20 years. One day she woke up and told me that she was no longer in love with me and wanted a divorce. Now, whenever I go on a date, she tries to sabotage it. What the fuck?"

Text seven...

He now looks at me and states that it's Tom and he has to text back.

Text eight...   Text nine...

Another phone call. He picked up the phone and by the sound of his voice, he was talking to Tom.

"Tom, you are 15 years old. Can't Harry's mom pick you up? I know I was just in Asia. But it is your

Mom's weekend." The phone call droned on five more minutes. Marvin was just not going to win this battle; I sensed it.

He hung up and gulped the remaining drops of his wine. I noticed I'd hardly sipped my own wine. I had been watching a major tennis match, and my neck was sore from following the volleys.

Text ten... Text eleven... Text twelve...

And the phone rang again and once again on cue Marvin picked that little smartphone up. A female voice was yelling at the top of her lungs. Marvin listened to her spew. He could not get in a word edge wise. He was nodding like a puppy. Marvin now looked 30 years older. His ass was being chewed by his ex-wife and his son was "guilting him to death" for his business trips to Asia. The two had managed to mangle our date from their mastery of manipulation. Marvin was drowning and I was just too numb to even throw him a life jacket. I motioned to Marvin that I needed to go to the bathroom. I was starving. I was ready to eat a snake. I was a wreck. I sat in the women's restroom pondering my next move. The Angel/Devil debate commenced:

ANGEL: You could stick it out and have dinner. Get to know him.

DEVIL: This is a waste of time. Bolt and you can still get a nice dinner in peace.

ANGEL: Marvin looks so pathetic, just be patient. It will all work out.

DEVIL: His ex-wife is a controlling bitch and his son is a brat. Run.

ANGEL: Just give him a chance. This too shall pass.

DEVIL: Pass my ass. The kid has another three years before he's 18, and the wife will sabotage every date you ever have. Don't kid yourself. He's just met you. If you were the chosen gal for Marvin, your life will be complete misery. The ex-wife will only make his life and your life hell. Cut being the "nice girl." This first date is a sign from me; get out now while you still can!

I walked out of the restroom and could see that Marvin was still on that damned phone. The rudeness factor was at an all-time high. And quite frankly, the Devil had won the debate. I smiled at Marvin and I motioned to the door.

"Marvin, this is just not working. I think it's best I leave."

He covered the receiver with his hand. "Can you wait one more second?" he pleaded.

"Marvin, no offense, but you really have your hands full. I don't think I'm ready to take on a guy that is sandwiched between his ex and his son. This is our very first date and you have taken 12 texts and 3 major phone calls and I haven't even eaten. So, sorry," I said as I turned on my heels and left. My boots were made for walking.

I found myself eating dinner that night at my favorite little bistro – The Cove Trattoria - by myself. No drama. No texts. No demanding manipulations, just a nice, quiet dinner for one. As I slowly masticated my penne bolognese, I realized I would be flying out of country to speak at a conference in the next month. Change would do me well. I welcomed the thought of going to my conference, promoting my team, and creating positive change with my upcoming lecture.

FROG NOTES: *Hop slowly onto the lily pad when the frog has tadpoles and an ex-princess in the bulrushes. Give yourself time to assess if you can handle the frog, his tadpole, **and** his ex. If you are a princess who wants lots of attention, best to get involved with a single frog that has no tadpoles.*

Conferences

The Business Conference—it is the place where you shake hands and pass out your best promotional material in order to build better business relationships. And, from my perspective, the perfect forum for sales people to travel away from home, drink a lot of alcohol, and revert to being in high school or college. Wow, they can be mentally and physically exhausting. I think of conferences as "survival of the fittest."

My goal at a convention is to network and learn as much as I can from the seminars. I go to every lecture and breakout session because I have this intrinsic need to gain more knowledge. I am amazed at what happens at conferences, and could write a whole book on the subject. I had already observed the results of dating a colleague from a conference, and had no intentions of going there myself.

The first day of conference observations:

- ❖ People have "escaped" reality. No kids, no spouse, no significant other—freedom, and the bar is open for business! And I mean wide open.

❖ Men and women dress to impress. Decked out to the nines. And some of the "business attire" resembled "eveningwear" or "lady-of-the-evening wear." And the stench of colognes exasperating.

❖ Attendees rationalize a conference as a "license to be out of control." What happens in Vegas stays in Vegas, right? Or they shout, "You only live once!"

❖ I'm sure most of the men (and women) who are married have taken off their wedding rings and probably say, "My spouse and I are having a really difficult time."

❖ After four hours of drinking at the bar, the conference attendees lose all control. In fact, one attendee admitted to smoking a huge doobie and was ready to party. *How attractive!*

At conferences, people hand out promotional materials to their colleagues so you'll remember them. They tend to get a little creative, if not completely out there. One man was handing out stuffed crabs. His goal: "All I want is to take a picture of the crab over your private parts and post it on Facebook." Really?

It was painful for this introverted extrovert to perform 100% at a convention laced with lots of alcohol and the "free" attitude. The whole experience was wearing on me. I love being a realtor, but the BS meter there was off the charts. The insincere compliments and the pick-up lines just got worse as each day turned into night. After 48 hours, my skin felt invaded by maggots. I woke early to work out in the fresh air just so I could breathe.

I knew I was in trouble when I was the guest speaker. For some crazy reason, some of my peers thought I had graduated to "celebrity" status. They elevated me on a pedestal and thought my words were dogma. Jesus. That was far from the truth. I just wanted to flash them my freckles and smack them into reality. I was still me. I just don't get stage fright. I love public speaking and love to share out-of-the-box ideas.

I approach all conferences the same way. I lugged out two bags: one was my 7'x4' display photo of my team; the other contained promotional materials. This year, I offered a "stress-o-meter" as a promotional gift. The stress-o-meter measured your stress level by holding your thumb on the index of the card and the result is a color. Green or blue means your stress level is normal, orange indicates moderate stress, but most people at the conference tested black, which meant they were under huge stress. To me, black indicated that most of my peers' moral compasses were off kilter and their guilt was registering on the card.

Stan approached me at my booth like an eager beaver. "Kris, I am so excited to hear you speak," he said as he offered his hand for a quick handshake. I could sense he was a bit nervous.

I shook Stan's hand firmly and said, "Thank you. I'm just glad to be here. Hopefully, some of the information will be helpful to you."

"I'm sure it will be. Do you mind if I take some of your cards?" Stan asked as he took a handful.

Stan was 6 feet tall and he epitomized "metrosexual." He was clearly the top dresser at the conference. His attire was perfectly color-coordinated and all his jewelry matched his outfit. He had the perfect tan. I even asked him on one occasion how he could be so tan? He responded, "I work on it." My private thought was, That means you hardly work. Obviously, he was a stickler for what he ate; he had less than 10% body fat for sure. He also had great posture and incredible Italian shoes.

Lunch came around quickly. It was ten per table so ears were open. Stan decided it was best to sit at my left. All the attendees at the table did what all conference attendees do best: pass the biz cards around and share war stories. Stan thought it would be a great idea to whip out a few stories immediately about his most recent divorce. Mind you, the recent divorce included his ex-wife, who was also a conference attendee and happened to be sitting five tables away. "My ex is a cunt," Stan blurted.

Whoa! Now that was not an appropriate noun to say to nine other people who have no idea who you are, and have not even broken bread with you!

Stan droned on about his rough divorce. He droned on to the point of nausea. In fact, I actually kicked him under the table and gave him my best stink-eye stating, "Stan, perhaps you should give the whole divorce thing a break. Let's move onto another topic!"

I might have been brutally honest, but I expressed something that most people were thinking. No matter what conference I have attended, my peers hear everything. They were just praying Stan would spill the beans on something they could use against him in business. I actually felt sympathy for Stan and just wanted his temporary insanity to stop.

Lunch came and went. Thank God. I moved on to breakout sessions and furthering my learning.

Stan became fixated on me. Better word: obsessed. He thought it would be a great idea to text me eight times in a two-hour period.

YOU HAVE TOUCHED MY HEART
YOU ARE SO BRAVE.
I WOULD FOLLOW YOU ANYWHERE.

YOU ARE SUCH A STRONG AND BEAUTIFUL WOMAN.

WOW.

LOL.

XOXO.

☺

I decided to just ignore these texts. In fact, texting just bothers me unless the user really knows how to communicate. All the acronyms and smiley faces are overused and trite. This guy barely knew me and he was texting me hugs and kisses. Ugh!

Time passed and my speaking debut had arrived. Stan arrived 15 minutes early to get a seat. He positioned himself right in front of the podium in the front row. He waved at me to make sure I saw him. I managed to smile, but I felt really awkward.

As I spoke to the crowd, Stan nodded at every word I said. He waved constantly. He resembled the male version of Glenn Close from the movie, Fatal Attraction. In fact, I am sure he would have made "rabbit stew" for me if he had the chance. He was laughing at all my jokes, clapping when I made an emphatic statement. He clapped when I was finished. And he was the only person in the entire ballroom to give me a standing ovation. Oh, God, even I knew I was not that good!

After my presentation, I was knee-deep in people who wanted to ask me questions. All I could hope for was that this line-up killed any hope for Stan to stick around. Unfortunately, his "doe" eyes were glazed over. He was going to wait out the crowd. My eyes darted around the room for the exit doors. After the last brave soul had asked his question, Stan still stood proud. He was lingering to talk to me.

"Great job, Kris. You were amazing," Stan said. I appreciated his compliment, but I looked at my watch and told him I was invited to a private dinner.

"Can I tag along?" Stan asked boldly.

"Unfortunately, it's a private dinner."

Stan persisted, "Perhaps, we can meet for a nightcap?"

OK, let me be clear here, hell no! He was recently divorced, he spoke unkindly of his ex in public, he was way too metrosexual for my taste and, most importantly, I would never again hook-up with anyone in my same profession. We parted ways and I headed off for more exhausting networking, small-talk, glasses of wine, and dinner. By the end of a full day of conferencing, I was totally socially depleted. I just wanted to go back to my hotel room and decompress. When I got back to my room, the little red light on my phone was flashing. A message awaited my attention. My heart rate increased as I heard the message. It was Stan.

"Kris, if it's not too late for you, perhaps you can visit me in my room. I'm in room 2102."

I erased the message, decided not to respond, washed my face and slipped into my comfy jammies for a good night's sleep. Prior to diving into the pillows, I quickly skimmed the 200 emails that were on my computer. Stan had emailed me eight times in one day. Conference Stalker! My natural skill for nipping something in the bud kicked into overdrive.

I emailed Stan back:

Dear Stan,

You are very good at what you do. I appreciate all your kindness and sincere compliments. I have a rule in my business life and it is simply this: I just do not fish off the company pier. I hope you will understand. May your business continue to thrive.

All the best,

Kris

Done. The Heavenly Bed pillow felt good against my head as I drifted off to a sound sleep.

I knew that when I got back to Arizona, I would be open to meeting local people. I was just going to go back and let karma take care of me. I would meet someone in the right place at the right time, if it was meant to be.

FROG NOTES: *Beware of the jumping frog who likes to play on many different lily pads! When jumping frogs pond hop, they will never return as the same frog. If you decide to keep him, get him tested.*

The Second Date

Getting to a second date is akin to climbing a very high mountain. You have struggled to get to the top and you feel pretty good, but your "euphoric buzz" is temporary. You still have to go back the same way you came up and, in many cases, most injuries happen on the way down.

Somewhere around Date #236, I found a frog that was worthy of a second date. I had met "Opie" while waiting in line at the post office. We struck up casual conversation in line and Opie asked me out for lunch the same week. Our first date was at a great little sandwich shop. Opie, who resembled the adult version of Andy's son from "The Andy Griffith Show," had passed my first date checklist: he had to be kind, unselfish, employed, and I had to have some physical attraction to the guy. Opie seemed well-mannered, backed by the fact he pulled out my chair for me on our first date and (bonus points) he did not lick his fingers after the appetizer was devoured.

He had a full-time job as a designer (I Googled him prior to meeting in person). He shared custody of his two boys with his ex-wife, which warmed me up to the idea that he wouldn't be a selfish Grinch. He was 6'5", which is important to a tall woman like me, and I was attracted to his red hair, nice smile and big, green eyes.

Opie boasted of being an avid hiker. Bonus points again for athleticism. On our first date, he willingly confessed, "Kris, I am a man who wears my heart on my sleeve." Wow, a man with feelings.

The second date was going to be a hike—a difficult trek in Sedona, Arizona, called Black Bear Trail. Sedona is a two-hour drive from Scottsdale, where I reside. Opie offered to pick me up but, since this was only our second date, I convinced him to meet me at a Fry's parking lot instead. As I arrived at 6:00AM, I noticed his Monster Truck; a white "badass" machine that boasted a rifle rack in the rear window, and hadn't had a bath for at least two dust storms.

I took in a deep breath and managed to blurt out, "Hello, Opie. Are you all ready for our hike?"

"Absofuckinglutely," Opie eagerly retorted. Wow, the "f" bomb at 6:00AM. Classy! He never cursed on our first date. I guess he saves that for special occasions.

I guess his cursing woke me up because I finally noticed Opie's attire for our venture: Camouflage army pants, a bright banana colored t-shirt, a fedora (a la Raiders of the Lost Ark that was trendy some 30 years ago), green rimmed sunglasses, and big hiking boots with red laces. Oh, my. I am no fashionista, but bright yellow was not the best color choice for this fair-skinned, redheaded, Ron Howard look-alike.

I took a running leap to get up into the "Monster" ride. As I adjusted into my seat, my eyes scanned my surroundings. Gum wrappers and used Kleenex on the floor, loose change in the console, two pine-scented tree-shaped air-fresheners hanging from his rearview mirror, and McDonald's bags (that I swear probably contained leftover Big Macs).

At this point in the story, it would probably be better to just get to the hike, but who can leave out the two-hour truck ride? My mind just cut to the chase. How can anyone drive a monster truck using his knee to steer? What is up with tailgating; do you need to be that close to read the bumper stickers? Do grown men over 40 really like Barry Manilow? And when someone sneezes five times in a row, wouldn't it be proper to grab a clean Kleenex?

We arrived at our hike and I literally left my body. My heart rate shot up to 180; I was in no mood to talk (in fact, I ground down my bottom teeth while gritting them during the long, long drive). My mission was simple: Get the hike and date over as soon as possible. For the record, Black Bear Trail normally takes the average hiker four hours to do. I am not a marathon runner, but my Irish was fired up! We were going to make it in record time.

While I walked in silence, Opie wanted to talk the whole time. The only words I could muster were, "Shhhh. I just want to take in nature." I was walking so fast, I was breathing like I was about to pass out. I could barely see with the sweat pouring into my eyes making nature one big blur. My gazelle stride was working, though, and I barely took any breaks. We completed the hike (and the majority of our date) in 2.5 hours. VICTORY! I sped towards the monster truck. The sooner I got in that garbage can on wheels, the sooner I would be home.

"Kris! Way to go man, you rock! You said you were athletic, but that is the best time I have ever had up here. For your reward, I would love to take you to this great little hole-in-the-wall Mexican restaurant," he offered. Urgg, some reward.

My stomach grumbled. I decided to ignore the fact that he just called me "man" and took him up on his offer. Besides, after all the calories we just burned, I worried that if I did not get some food, I might just kill him on the way home.

The chips and salsa could not go down any faster. As my blood sugar normalized, my keen observation skills kicked in. Opie decided he needed an oversized margarita to replenish his electrolyte loss. Well, by then it was already 11:00AM. It has got to be 5:00pm somewhere. Go for it, Opie.

I watched him slurp down his alcoholic version of Gatorade and began zeroing in on him and his eating habits. I began a one-sided conversation with him in my mind: Is that dirt under your fingernails as you shove the salsa we have been both sharing into your mouth? Is it polite to talk with food in your mouth? When you get to the bottom of the glass, do you really need to slurp? It must be a great meal if refried beans land not only on the banana-yellow t-shirt but your camouflage pants, too.

After the trough was destroyed by man consumption, Opie smiled at me. He reached for my hand across the table and said, "Kris, I have never met anyone like you. I told you I wear my heart on my sleeve and I just want you to know... I think I love you."

OMG! Absofuckinglutely NOT. I could not believe what I'd heard. My hand snapped away from his like a slingshot. My "outdoor" voice erupted, "Opie, you hardly know me. This is only our second date. I think it's time we wrap up lunch and head back to Scottsdale." I was beyond uncomfortable at this point. And then it happened. That situation all women dread.

A tear rolled down Opie's cheek as he quivered, "But, you are the one for me. I just know it. I have been waiting a long time for this. I feel we have this incredible chemistry." He warbled on, but I was in absolute shock. Yes, he did say he wore his heart on his sleeve, but seriously? Time to snap him out of it; I decided psychobabble would be my only hope since I had to survive a two-hour ride home with this softie.

"Opie, you were divorced only five months ago. I think you are projecting what you want onto me. We really don't know each other. You are a nice man, but this is just too sudden for all this feeling. How about I make this deal with you: we can talk more about all this as I drive us back to Scottsdale?"

Opie agreed. And I was relieved as he slid me his keys. He was still teary eyed as we jumped up into the monster truck.

"I thought we had something special, but I guess not," he finally replied. His passive-aggressive side reared its ugly head. "And after all I have done for you."

All I could think at that point was this "man-boy" could be the Ted Bundy type. He could whip out a huge machete from under his messy seat, cut me up into small pieces, and who would know where to find me? I decided that no commentary was the best bet now that he showed his true self.

He finally turned his shoulder to me and stared out the passenger window. Opie resembled a pouting child who dropped his candy. The silence was deafening, but short-lived. Soon, Opie was snoring as he passed out from all the drama and his massive margarita. I sighed in relief knowing that this date would soon end. The Fry's parking lot resembled my pot of gold as we neared it. I turned off the ignition and handed Opie his keys.

He was still not in the mood to talk, but upon my exit he stated: "Kris, you will really regret this. We had something special. I know you will think about me. You could have had a really good thing."

I simply smiled and wished him the best.

And then... I gazelle-sprinted to my car.

"Celebration" by Kool and the Gang played on the radio. I could not help myself. I turned the song up full-blast as I skidded out of the parking lot and sang along.

Travel would do me good. I was actually excited to get out of town after this nightmare of a second date. I looked forward to my next speaking engagement.

FROG NOTES: *Best to drive your own coach to your second date, Cinderella. Never stray far from your own lily pad in case your frog turns into a toad. And make sure your Fairy Godmother knows your exact location of your date in case you need to be rescued.*

Airports and Planes

For the record, I am not Angelina Jolie or Sophia Loren. When a photographer once asked me to "act sexy" for the camera, I started to laugh hysterically. My mother has always described me as having a "kind face" with a good smile that makes people feel good. So, whenever I am in an airport or on an airplane, it never ceases to amaze me how men I do not know feel the need to open up to me. It is almost like they feel compelled to talk to me.

I think of a plane as a large bus in the sky. Neither an airport nor planes are ideal "dating igniters" for me. Heck, I am a nervous flyer. Plus, over time I have acquired a loathing for long-distance relationships. So, when Jennifer encouraged me to be more open to the idea of meeting a stranger on a plane, I remained 'skenical' (my homemade word for being skeptical and cynical about an idea), but I agreed to try.

The night before a trip, I am usually restless. My overactive mind goes through gobs of checklists of what I need to bring, accomplish and do before, during, and after the trip. And it always seems that business picks up right before I leave town, so I am in "intense focus" mode before I even pack.

The morning of a flight, I have usually accomplished more than a person gets done in a week. I strategically pack to be Miss Efficient. Getting through security as fast as possible becomes my mission. Eighty percent of the time, I carry luggage on the plane, but for conferences, I have all of my materials to check in.

The morning of this trip, I felt great! I had gone to spin class, emailed 42 clients, spoken to the people I care about on the phone, and I was now in line to check my bags.

"So, little lady, where you heading today?" said someone in the check-in line.

I whipped around to acknowledge the cowboy voice behind me. As I turned, I got a whiff of cigarette cologne. I also registered a hint of Jim Beam mixed with the stench of smoke. My eyes quickly scanned the Marlboro Man. He was probably 20 years my senior and was wearing Ostrich boots, Levis, and a bright orange shirt. His eyes were blood shot and I noticed that he has broken blood vessels around his nose.

"I am heading to a conference in Washington, DC. And you?" I inquired. I looked at the check-in line and it was moving. I figured I'd have about two minutes of small-talk with Marlboro Man, and then we'd both be off on our own merry, separate ways.

"Well, darlin', I am heading to Michigan to hunt for a couple of days. Then, spend a few more days fishing."

Aha! No wonder he wore a bright orange shirt. I was not surprised he was a fisherman too. I observed his fingernails – and the dirt lodged under them. He rambled on, "I just spent time with my daughter. Hell, she needs a better beer supply and, for that matter, she needs to choose better wine." Now I knew why he owned those broken blood vessels around his nose.

He continued, "Prior to visiting her, I went to a super drug convention. It was outstanding."

STOP... RIGHT... THERE...

Notation: I know being a complete stranger makes you feel like you have the liberty to tell me everything. But, if you are trying to "chat up" a woman, best to keep quiet on the following topics:

- ❖ Your recent drug use;
- ❖ Your desire for sex three or more times a day with multiple partners;
- ❖ Your addiction to various pornography sites;
- ❖ Your need to drink from 8AM onward, announcing that, "it's five o'clock somewhere";
- ❖ Your gambling habit, which translates to losing more than you earn;
- ❖ Your fondness for little girls;

Kissing Frogs: Tall Tales and Insights From the Dating Pond

- Your fondness for sheep or other animals; or
- Your membership to numerous dating sites (both for married and single seekers).

I was saved by the shrill voice of a disgruntled airline employee. "Next!" she shouted. I darted to my kiosk. I checked my baggage and no more Marlboro Man.

Next up: Security Line...

Have you ever noticed people in the security line? They know they are going to have to strip off shoes, remove laptops, and get their four ounce liquids out. Why do they dress with lace up shoes? Why do they pack their laptop underneath 18 books, notepads and magazines? Why do they insist on dumping their liquids out of their purses or man-satchels and then decide to place them in a zip lock bag? As you can tell, I appreciate being organized. My nerves get shot by people's inability to have the foresight for the security line. The line should move quickly. Really? Plan ahead and move the line forward! Yes, I am the poster girl for patience. Not!

But, I guess that is why my friend Jennifer loves the airport. These delays provide the woman ample opportunity to meet a man and a potential love match. Barf!

Jesse was standing in front of me in the security line. He was 10 years my junior wearing jeans, a light pink Oxford shirt, a lime green 'skinny' tie, and some cool looking black loafers. His hairstylist could be Robert Pattison's. He had a black, leather man-satchel that housed his iPad, and he was texting furiously on his iPhone. While he keyed in a few more texts, the line moved but he did not. So, I bumped into him slightly. After all, I wanted to get through security and get to my plane. He turned around quickly, clearly perturbed. I had grazed his metrosexual being.

I smiled and said, "Oops…I am so sorry."

His face relaxed, "I'll live."

Silence.

He gave me the once-over. His eyeballs gawked at me from my toes to my head and I felt like a big piece of meat. Awkward! He shrugged. "Hi, I'm Jesse. Where are you heading today?" I told him that I was off to speak in Washington, DC.

"Are you going to Dulles or Reagan?" Jesse asked, and I let him know Reagan would be my final destination. "What a coincidence, I'm going there too." Jesse's smile got a little bigger and my new friend had managed to snap his iPhone back on his waist. For the time being, his texting was backseat to the conversation. We made small-talk about where we worked, where we were born, and how we both liked living in Arizona.

We managed to move slowly through security. When I took off my boots for the scan, I noted that I was the same height as Jesse with his shoes off. Good. He whipped out his iPad and he had pre-packed his liquids. He was not holding up the line. Good. I watched Jesse push back his left sleeve to remove his watch and that is when I get a glimpse of…a tattoo! Hmmm… Now, I wondered what art might be hiding under his shirt and pants. I thought his tattoo had a hint of eagle or bird to it. God, I hate birds. Come to think of it, eagles have huge beaks. Had I ever dated anybody with a tattoo? What would my Dad think? OK, Kris. Slow down. You are in the security line. Breathe.

Jesse waited for me to get through the scanner and we walked to our gate. I asked more questions of Jesse and learned he was one of four kids, he owned a yellow Labrador, his favorite movie was Braveheart, and his favorite color was green. I also learned that I was the only person asking questions. This conversation was very one-sided—it was all about Jesse.

As we approached our gate, our plane had already boarding passengers. Jesse was in the "A" group and I was in the "B". He told me he would save me a seat. Now I was in a pickle! Did I just commit to sitting next to him? Do I even like him? This is a four-hour flight, Kris. God, I hate feeling trapped. Jesse was in aisle seven and he seemed way too eager. He motioned to me as I entered the plane. I just nodded.

There was a saving grace. He was sitting in the aisle seat and both the middle and window seats were still open. I grabbed the window seat. Jesse was a bit taken-aback by the fact I did not sit right next to him. He grabbed his iPhone and began to

text as I settled into my seat. The flight attendant mentioned to us that the flight would be full. I sat still in my seat like a little lamb. I occupied myself with reorganizing my organizer and avoided Jesse's gaze because I was not feeling a connection. In fact, I was rationalizing the following:

- ❖ I was 10+years older than Jesse.
- ❖ What could I possibly have in common with him?
- ❖ Does he want children?
- ❖ Does he play X-Box games?
- ❖ What if his whole body is full of tattoos?
- ❖ Why did I sit here?
- ❖ I could have just avoided eye contact and kept moving to aisle 14 or 21.
- ❖ Jesus, help me.

And then Rachel appeared. She was 15 years younger than I am. She was very petite, with long, brown hair and big, brown eyes. She resembled Selena Gomez. And all I could think was that junior just met his true match.

They yakked and giggled the four hours of the flight. As we hit Reagan's tarmac and pulled into the gate, I could tell that there had been a love match. As I grabbed my laptop bag and purse, I felt a hand tug my jacket.

"Hey, Kris, it was great to meet you. Thanks for taking the window seat," Jesse said.

I just smiled as one of my favorite quotes from my Grandpa passed through my head, "Sometimes things just work out the way they are supposed to work out."

After landing in Washington, DC, I received a voicemail from my friend, Anne, who encouraged me to join her for line-dancing on Saturday night. A glass of wine and some dancing would be great after my speaking trip.

FROG NOTES: When a frog is too eager and clingy, and all is moving too fast, cut bait. Sometimes the frog in the pond is better off with another princess.

Divorced Man with Kids
One More Time- Date #262

You would think that I would never go out again with a divorced man with kids, but heck, that's 60% of the single male population. I just had to remember that there are three components to put in the back of the skullcap: The ex-wife, the kids themselves and, perhaps, the in-laws. What else could possibly go wrong?

Ron was a Director of Athletics for a huge subdivision of homes in my area. In fact, over 25,000 people live in that massive development. The rumor-mill actually had it that it was akin to a "small town where people swing to make their lives more fun."

Ron had been divorced twice, and his most recent divorce was five months before I'd met him. He had three kids from his first wife (two boys and a girl), and adopted a baby girl with his second wife. Ron was a former pro-hockey player; he had charisma and always greeted people with a smile. He had one dog, and he loved watching or playing hockey with his two teenage boys.

I had met Ron at a country-western bar. Everyone was line-dancing, and I was the wallflower at the bar waiting for my friend, Anne, to show up for a glass of wine. To my surprise, Anne never showed up.

Ron and I chatted until about 10:00pm. He wanted to know what I did and where I worked. A few days later, I had a voicemail from Ron wondering if I would be open to a dinner with him. I called Ron back and, within five days, we had our first date, which would be my 313th. We were going to meet for dinner halfway between his Swingtown and my hometown. We chose a neutral spot about 25 miles away from my home.

We had good conversation and a nice dinner. He did not bite his fingernails or text during dinner, which was different from some of my previous dates. He seemed polite, courteous and funny, and had good stories to share. He and I laughed a great deal. It was a good date; nothing spectacular, but nothing hideous. We decided to go on a second date. I even agreed to a third and fourth date. We were having fun, but nothing was serious. We were enjoying the lightness of dating and I was taking it **slowly.** Ron mentioned that he and his first wife were having problems with his middle son. He was also struggling to make child support payments to his second wife. I was still taking it **slowly.**

On the fifth date, Ron wanted me to meet his 13-year-old daughter, Ronnie. Ironically, Ronnie was named after Ron. She was athletic and had been feeling a bit jilted from having wife number one and wife number two leave her life. I said to Ron, "We haven't dated all that long. Are you absolutely sure that this will be a good thing, me meeting Ronnie this soon?" My intuition just shrieked, Kris, do not do this! He emphasized that meeting her would be the best thing in the world.

I absolutely adored Ronnie. She was more than he could have described. She was beautiful, kind, gracious, giving, and she exuded great passion. Her whole existence was to make Ron happy. She wanted her dad to have love in his life.

On the fifth date, I jumped in the pool with Ronnie and the dog. We played hide and seek. I braided her hair. I just thought she was the best kid I had ever met. On the sixth date, Ron started to tell me some things that set off **red flags**.

"Kris, I'm just going to mail my keys to the bank and let it go into foreclosure."

"My one son is addicted to coke."

"Do you think I can borrow $2,000.00? I promise to pay it back."

"If things don't work out with my re-fi, can Ronnie and I move in with you?"

Did I hear that right? So, I went into logic mode. The legalities of a short sale and foreclosure I could handle. A son on coke? Perhaps I could handle that with the right counselor. Borrow $2,000.00? Perhaps, but I would need to probe deeper. But, can Ronnie and I move into your house after six dates? Hell, NO!

I was not ready for a man and his daughter (no matter how wonderful she is) to move in with me. I had no idea what kind of guy he was. I hadn't met his parents let alone seen how he managed his day-to-day life. How could I go from jumping in a pool with his daughter to having the both of them living in my personal space every day of my life, and the other children every other weekend? Moving in with a man and kids was a **huge step**.

I came up with a soft response. "Ron, we are still courting one another and it is too soon to even talk about living together."

Ron was quite devastated. "But, I need your help," he yelped.

I shared that I understood his need for help, but that he and I need more time to develop our relationship. Taking on the financials of him and his children was a major decision. And I was starting to sweat and feel suffocated.

"Kris, I think you're not being open," Ron stated confidently. "Ronnie really cares for you and this would be a really good thing."

Déjà-Vu. I have heard this statement before. Some man who thinks I can save the day. Some guy who has been to my house once and now thinks I can give him an escape route. I was absolutely a wreck. Heck, the more I thought about it, the more I realized I cared more for Ronnie than I did Ron.

All of a sudden, I felt that I was being put in the role of Sugar mama? I was ticked. I was appalled. I was ready to eat Ron's jugular vein!

"Riddle me this Ron—when you walked me to my car the first night, did you make note of what kind of car I drove? When you came to my home for the first time, did you mentally start placing your furniture in the empty spaces? When you saw me with Ronnie, did you even care about me or whether I offered something to Ronnie?"

Go figure, I managed to spew more. "Ron, do you even like me. Or do you just like what you think I can do for you? (Pause) More importantly, what are you willing to offer me, Ron?"

I waited for his answer…

And waited…

Ron remained silent.

My mind raced to the evenings with my "spin" friends and how everyone chirps their philosophy, and all I can hear is this meandering thought, Beware the person who wants you to make them a priority, when all you are is their option.

I was feeling sick. I must have appeared to be Ron's savior. Perhaps he saw me as his meal ticket, his room and board. I was a good role model for his daughter, but Ron was desperate. And desperate men who are in financial disarray are dangerous!

Not all divorced men with kids have this same problem. The truth be told, it was going to take me a long time to accept all the "baggage" that accompanies the ex-wives, the multiple kids, and drama that come with a fractured family. I would need time to observe the father with his kids; how he functioned with his exes; and how I would interact with his kids. I mean, a woman dating a divorced man with kids needs to actually like the man she is dating; and she needs to know if she can actually get along with his kids, not to mention their moms. All this takes time, and for some ex-hockey pro with a good smile to think all of this cannot be forced on me too much, too fast. Forcing me into a corner only exerts one option for me: Bolt! Hell, bolt quickly.

My phone call was simple: "Hi, Ron, it's Kris. I know I should do this in person, but time is important to me. I know things are rough for you right now with your home. I have given a lot of thought to having you and Ronnie move in with me but, I am not ready for that. I never even had sex with you. I have never talked to you about anything important. We have just started dating. I feel really pressured right now and this is just not working out for me."

Ron sighed, "Wow. That is too bad. I was hoping that things would be different. I wish you the best. But, I need to do what's most important for my family."

I never heard from Ron or Ronnie again. Rumor has it that Ron is married to his third wife and has another adopted kid.

I am amazed at how the lightness of dating turned sour so quickly. I amazed myself at ignoring some major flags for some "fun" times. Note to self: Kris, look at the full image, not just the "cropped" photo.

FROG NOTES: Look closely at the frog that has a lot of baggage. What does the frog with tadpoles offer you? Perhaps you are a princess nightingale who just wants to "save" broken frogs.

The Crop Shot

In the digital age, it's easy to alter an image. We don't always get to see the full picture. Usually, we just see what someone wants us to. Sometimes, we only see what we want to.

A "crop shot" is one way to explain the male photo in your mind—you maximize it to its most aesthetic image. You mentally "crop out" any negatives that might be around this new man in your life. You "crop out" all the external stimuli that hinder the beauty of the image.

In dating or courtship, all people have this great "crop shot" image of the person they are seeing. For women, we tend to project potential on most of the men we meet, and "crop out" all the other flags that are raised in the first 90 days of dating. Sometimes, we just "force a square peg into a round hole" due to loneliness, lack of sex, the thought of having something "new" in our lives, or the man is actually paying attention to us for a brief period of time.

I can honestly say that I have been a true "cropper." Let's not forget the chapter where it took me months to figure out what my long-distance hero's full image was. My crop of him was all about his good looks, charm and success. His full image was small-town boy without a formal education, ability to call a double-wide trailer a "beach house", his infidelity, and his need to have his ego recognized and gratified.

Let's look at other **crops** that have taken place over the years and what the **full image** that bubbled to the surface looks like:

CROP SHOT: The man is so caring and thoughtful because he texts two or more times a day. (Note the word 'text'.) Because of this, he is considered a "true communicator." If he also manages to type out two sentences in a 24-hour period, he is deemed the "ultimate communicator."

THE FULL IMAGE: He still has not picked up the phone to call you. He hides behind one-way, brief, Twitter-like communication, which is as deep as his vocabulary will allow.

CROP SHOT: The man is so handsome. He has a great physique, perfect teeth and he clearly takes good care of himself. We are obsessed with his looks.

THE FULL IMAGE: He's still a momma's boy. He calls his mom a dozen times each day, and she still does his laundry. When you look closely, he has veneers. His eyes have been lifted. And he works way too hard on his tan. His IQ is around 90. He is the true male Barbie.

CROP SHOT: The man is a sexual dynamo, a true Casanova in the bedroom. He puts foreplay on the map for you. You have literally been to the moon and back when you are with him, doing things you never even thought were possible (or legal). You have never experienced the ecstasy this man brings to the bedroom.

THE FULL IMAGE: He is a sex addict. He is addicted to porn and cannot keep his Johnson in his pants. In fact, he is the narcissist that will never settle down. He has never been married OR he has been married multiple times and the reason for his divorces is his "wandering dick syndrome."

CROP SHOT: The man bowls you over as super sensitive because he worships his kids. He shows you their photos on his phone. You are amazed that he is such a "family man." He gushes about them all the time!

THE FULL IMAGE: He works incessantly and he never sees his kids. The true caretakers to his children are his ex, his nanny, his mother and his mother-in-law. His kids barely know him and, boy, do they resent him.

CROP SHOT: The man has just suffered losing his wife **or** he's been recently divorced or dumped. He is so sad. In fact, he needs you to help him get his life together—cook his meals, get his house back in order and help him with daily tasks. He tells you of his tragic loss and you feel so sorry for him, so of course you help him any way you can.

THE FULL IMAGE: He and his wife were fighting before her death/divorce/breakup. He inherited a **huge** life insurance policy upon her death **or** he was awarded alimony in the divorce. Or, if he just broke up, he inherited freedom. He is the true **victim** mongrel who is always blaming someone else and soon he will blame you, too.

CROP SHOT: The man is a communicator. He shows interest in you by asking you lots of questions. You are shocked that he is this genuinely interested in you. He wants to see you every day.

THE FULL IMAGE: He was recently laid off and he has more time on his hands than he's ever had. You are a sugar mama to him. He would love to move into your home and help "lighten your load."

CROP SHOT: He is a renaissance man. He can paint, write, tango, dance, sing, work, play golf at a six handicap, loves theater, wine, dining; he is a dream come true. He woos you with his cornucopia of talents.

THE FULL IMAGE: He woos **all** women with his talents. He has no desire to settle down. You are his muse for the moment.

CROP SHOT: The man can listen. You never thought you would meet someone who would actually "get" you. He hears every word you say and can repeat it all back to you with clear understanding. He never seems bored. He just wants to know about you.

THE FULL IMAGE: He had a felony arrest for possession. His temper flares when he drinks too much. He has been known to "snap" and put his girlfriend's head in a choke hold. *Lovely!*

CROP SHOT: The man is so funny; he could be a professional comedian. His sarcastic wit is alluring. You have never had so much fun in your life!

THE FULL IMAGE: He is an alcoholic. He starts drinking at 8:00AM at the closest watering hole. If he does not drink, he gets the shakes. When he's not drunk, he is cynical and rude.

CROP SHOT: The man is sincere. He has all the right things to say. He loves his mom and dad. He believes that people should get a fair shake in life if they work hard. He eats apple pie. He just seems to be grounded *and* he has morals.

THE FULL IMAGE: He is a Trust-a-farian, living off his parents' money. He has never worked a day in his life. He spends his time watching ESPN, CNN, CSPAN, FOX News, and all the home shopping channels. He does not give to charity. And his house is a pigsty (why spend that trust fund on a maid?).

CROP SHOT: He is Mr. Benevolent. He is very religious and believes in giving to the community. You are bowled over by his goodness, and all the worthy causes he supports.

THE FULL IMAGE: He loves to see himself in print and receive awards. He lives for the recognition, not to give for the sake of giving.

CROP SHOT: The man is generous, a giver. He buys you presents, calls you three times a day and he's there for you whenever you need him there. He wants to see you every single night. He is "Johnny on the Spot."

THE FULL IMAGE: He is lonely and has no friends. His preoccupation is YOU. You've become his world and focus.

CROP SHOT: The man is a charmer. He owns the room when he walks into it. He makes you feel like you are the most wonderful person in the world. He exudes charisma and just oozes compliments.

THE FULL IMAGE: He cannot feel. He does not possess empathy. He wants you to like him but, in truth, he has shut his heart down. He is numb. He loves to flirt, but the reality is he floats from woman to woman because he cannot allow himself to be close to **anyone**. He loses control if he gets too close. His persona has been built on keeping people feeling good, but at a distance.

Being **aware** of and avoiding the crop shot is the first step to dating success. The full image will eventually surface. And, after five years of dating, I was ready for the real picture.

FROG NOTES: If he looks like a frog, acts like a frog, and smells like a frog, no amount of kissing is going to turn him into a prince.

The Knight in Shining Armor (KISA)

As a damsel in distress, one hopes for the "Knight in Shining Armor" to save her from the ugly world of dating. I am hardly a "Cinderella", and I definitely think "Sleeping Beauty" is a curse, but I am a hopeful romantic. I truly believed that I would meet a man who would be respectful, really have my back and be my life's companion. In fact, there are three words that describe my perfect Prince Charming: kind, intelligent and funny. And, funny as being **funny**— not kind of funny, but incredibly witty, slightly sarcastic and having the ability to laugh at himself.

Many men think they are funny, but their jokes fall flatter than a penny off the Empire State Building. Many men think they are kind, but they cannot read a woman when she needs empathy. Many men claim they are intelligent, but to me, intelligence has to be on two levels: cerebral **and** emotional. There are men that have a high IQ, but they lack the EIQ that really brings a woman to her knees. In fact, I have often thought of keeping the book Emotional Intelligence in the trunk of my car for my one-time dates that lack EIQ, so I can hand them the book and say, "Read this, it might help. Good luck to you!"

So, with much chagrin, I decided to go back to the online dating pond. The mere idea of it made my stomach do flip-flops. However, with all my dating experiences and observations, online seemed to be the best avenue for me to meet someone.

For me, the hardest part about online dating was posting my photos—and mind you, I do not have bikini photos, nor do I possess tattoos, and there are no "bust" shots for me to offer. If anything, I just look like the All-American girl next door. I appear "professional" in my tailored suits. I have a few photos of "casual" me in jeans and a sweater, and I have one action shot of me playing tennis so they could see that I am "athletic". I took the time to carefully write my profile and was clear on my boundaries:

"If you are looking for an IM/Texting partner, casual sex encounter, someone to swing with your wife, or if you are married/in a relationship/or separated, DO NOT contact me. If you are a casual or frequent drug or alcohol abuser, or you like to abuse women, DO NOT contact me."

I thought by including this in my profile up front, it would limit the amount of **freaks** that could possibly contact me. I also was very clear on what I look like, what I like to do, what I truly want in a relationship, and what I am willing to give in a relationship. I noticed that many profiles were vague and many had no clue as to what they wanted.

Unlike many of my friends, who tell me they get hundreds of winks and emails per day, my new and improved profile brought in just a few hits. Now, some would say a few hits lower your chances, but I like the idea of paying attention to the sender. Hell, three hits per day seemed outstanding to me. I was curious about their inquiries and immediately read their profiles. My process of elimination was simple: If he spent time and effort on his profile and pictures, he was worth time and effort in return.

One evening, there was an email from "Knightrider". He did not send a wink, which is just clicking a tab on Match.com that acts like a "Hello." All I could conjure up in my mind was, if you can wink, why not freaking email the woman and just start a conversation? Are you a wuss?

Knightrider was not a wuss. His email was simple, but came in loud and clear: "I enjoyed reading your profile and thought we had some things in common. Would you want to talk on the phone sometime? I would like to get to know you better." OK, hold your horses. There were no spelling errors. He actually wanted to talk on the phone. And he wanted to get to know me better? I immediately clicked on his profile.

His photos exhibited a very handsome man who appeared tall and very athletic with kind, bright blue eyes and dark hair. He was divorced with three boys (ages 10, 12 and 13); he enjoyed travel, good food and wine, hiking, skiing, time with family and friends, good conversation, and comedy. He was well put together with a good sense of style. It was obvious he bathed, and he had an incredibly infectious smile.

I scrolled through a few more pictures and made the assumption that he played piano and chess. But in one of his photos, he posed topless. I must say, I cringe at guys taking their shirts off to make a statement. But, if this guy was for real, his body was definitely photo-shopped at the gym. Truth be told, I had never seen a man in this good of shape my entire life. Knightrider was a bit overwhelming and a bit intimidating, I must say. If I ever had the opportunity to meet him in person, it would be my goal to poke his abs to see if his picture was the real deal.

I decided to email Knightrider back. I kept in mind that his profile stated that he wanted to be a Humphrey Bogart to an Ingrid Bergman. "Hello, Knightrider. I enjoyed your profile, too, and it would be great to talk on the phone. But, would you be okay with Katherine Hepburn instead of a Bergman?"

I am more like Katherine than Ingrid. Ingrid always had that weepy, distressed look and made a huge mistake leaving Bogey at the plane. Katherine would have played it differently. She would have been strong, sassy, and would have swept Humphrey onto the plane.

Knightrider and I set up a time to talk on the phone. We both knew it would be a test for the following:

- ❖ Do either of us have a mousy voice?
- ❖ Can we speak eloquently? If we set an exact time, will the other person be "on time"?
- ❖ Can we interact long enough to make it to the "in-person" date?

Our phone call was set for 10:00AM. We both passed the test and set a date to meet for a glass of wine at a cute bistro the following evening at 6:30.

The day of the big date, I was really excited. But, as fate would have it I had an emergency and needed to **cancel**. Crap! This was not the first impression I wanted to make, but this would be a tell-tale sign if he could hang in there with me. I asked if we could reschedule and Knightrider assured me that it was all OK, and we would reschedule our date for Friday night instead. Whew!

On Friday night, I was prompt at 6:30, waiting at the bar. I had already asked the bartender to pour Knightrider's favorite red wine.

"I'm running 10 minutes late," Knightrider's text read.

Normally, being a time-miser, I would have counted that as a red flag, but I was lenient since I botched our first meeting. So, I sipped my wine and studied the menu. Then, I felt this permeating energy enter the room. I turned, and there he was.

Knightrider was actually better in person than his photos. I think I was in complete shock as he took a seat next to me. He was confident, handsome and sexy as hell. I think I might have been drooling. I quickly sipped my wine to calm my giddy nerves.

"You must be Kris," he smiled. Now mind you, I could tell Knightrider was looking me over from head to toe to make sure I was not an alien.

"And you must be Ted," I said as we shook hands.

I felt instant attraction and connection! Ted was rapidly passing my dating guidelines and I had no crop shots of him. The last time I felt a connection like this was date #10. I was hoping this would turn out better.

He was confident; excellent posture, his limited hand movements while speaking to me, and the calmness of his voice proved that. I really think if a siren went off during our date, Ted would be the calmest person in the room, steady and assured.

Ted was funny as he shared a story of how when he was young and on vacation with his family, he and his youngest brother put shaving cream in Mad Dog's (their middle brother) hand while he was sleeping, then feathered his cheeks. Mad Dog awoke to shaving cream all over his face and immediately chased after Ted and his brother, who were hiding in the hotel bathroom. Mad Dog tried to breakdown the bathroom door while Ted called his mom in the other room, begging her to come and save their lives.

Ted praised his mother, as she was the glue in his life. He shared with me how his mom had been there through his divorce, helped him raise his boys, and how she volunteered at the local elementary school.

He gushed on about his three boys, who were smart, athletic, and had amazing energy. He attended every baseball game they played and assisted them with their school projects.

He asked poignant questions of me, even a few that were probing. He wanted to know about my business, my strengths, and what I really thought about online dating.

He was a business *winner*. I had Googled him prior to our meeting and he had run several successful business ventures. He shared with me insights to the entrepreneurial projects he was part of at the time.

He was respectful! He treated me as though I was the only woman in the room. Mind you, there were many beautiful women strolling by us, but he kept his eyes gazed on me.

He was kind. This kindness was expressed when he asked, "Are you hungry?" or "Kris, do you need anything?" I was pretty much shocked! Can we just clone him and sell him on eBay? I would make a fortune.

We talked for two hours and, at the end of the second hour, he asked if he could kiss me. I humbly obliged. Of course!

Now, here is the thing: If you kiss someone and nothing happens, I think you should call it a day. If you kiss someone and your heart skips a beat, then you might have something special. But, if someone kisses you and you feel a WOW—that is a wonderful and rare thing! His kiss was tender, and I felt a big WOW!

Ted then told that me he had to get back to his kids because it was his custody week. We shut down the tab and he walked me to my car. He kissed me again and asked if we could see each other on Sunday for a dinner date. He would arrange a sitter. And, of course, yours truly agreed to a second date with Ted.

I was just ecstatic that he was so kind, funny and intelligent. And he could kiss!

Between Friday and Sunday, Ted had texted me several messages and called once. He even sent me photos of him and his boys at the water park. We planned to meet at a beautiful resort with great views of the valley at 7:30pm for drinks on the veranda, and then mosey into the best steak restaurant in town for dinner.

I decided to pull out my turquoise cocktail dress. I didn't want to overdo it, but I did want to wear a color that would be charming and enchanting. I entered the veranda right on time with nervous energy, excited to see Ted again. I arrived first and chose a great table, then ordered myself a glass of champagne. I received a text from Ted: "Hey, running 10 minutes behind, but I am on my way."

I just focused on the sunset and the distant airplanes on their descent into Phoenix. What a beautiful night. What a great glass of champagne. What a gorgeous resort. He tapped me on the shoulder and I literally snapped back to reality.

Ted said, "You look beautiful." And, to be honest, I felt beautiful. He looked gorgeous, so I sputtered, "You look great, too." Time stopped. It was one of the best dates of my life!

Ted and I laughed. We shared our life stories and empathized with one another. I was just happy to spend time with another person who was real! It was great to be with someone I felt comfortable with (for the first time in so long), and it was nice to be able to be me. I was able to trust Ted. I just let go.

Ted and I enjoyed a wonderful year together. But, after many discussions, we have cooled off our relationship to see if we can handle timing issues. Ted needs to gain traction in his work life and I need to know if he has the emotional energy to give a relationship.

I am grateful for my time with Ted. Even though I have no idea at this point if this will be the "happily ever after" ending I was hoping for, this relationship opened my heart and set my mind to what I truly wanted from my future Prince Charming.

Will this be my final chapter or will Kris move onto date #413 #1? Father Time will tell all.

FROG NOTES: Some frogs you meet in your pond are knights in shining armor. They come into you your life for a reason, season or lifetime. Time will always chip away at their armor to reveal if he is truly your Prince Charming, or just a really nice guy who's not really meant for you. Live, love and learn.

About the Author

Kris Anderson is an author, blogger, and an Internet radio host for her talk show *The Dating Pond*. A top-producing Arizona realtor, who has appeared on HGTV's "House Hunters", Kris is a former professional tennis player who was inducted into the Athletic Hall of Fame at Loyola Marymount University, where she graduated with honors, earning a BA in Communications.

Kris is currently working on the follow up book to Kissing Frogs, *Interviews with Frogs—Live from the Lilly Pad.*

If you are interested in submitting your own dating stories to share in print, online or on the radio, please go to www.thedatingpond.com and click the "Submissions" link. We would love to hear from you: Your stories must be shared!

YOU deserve a little more FRITZ in your life...

Go to:
www.TheDatingPond.Com/fritz

Enter promo code
(FRITZ)
and gain access to
"*Getting Fritzed*' - fun
gifts and events to help you,
your friends peers and
daughters keep that SPARK
in dating!

www.ingramcontent.com/pod-product-compliance
Lightning Source LLC
LaVergne TN
LVHW021448080426
835509LV00018B/2206